THEY LURK
IN THE MURK:
HOME WATERS

BY

GAGE A PETERS

Paperback ISBN: 978-1-7379267-1-9
Hardcover ISBN: 978-1-7379267-2-6

For my parents, Monty and Lora Peters

CHAPTER 1

ABILENE

A long, flat field of golden grass flowed in the afternoon wind. The air was clean, the sky a deep, engulfing blue with not a cloud in sight. Cows grazed the field and swished their tails back and forth to keep the flies away. It stretched into the horizon and would seem like it never ended if not for a dirt road and barbed wire fence that cut through it.

A trail of off-white dust followed behind a two door Ford pickup truck as it bounced down the road. It parked off to the side, and a young man and woman jumped out. The man had thick, brown hair, which pointed in every direction from driving with the windows down, and the beginnings of a beard that was patchy and uneven. The woman had long brown hair that swayed in the wind, with eyes that matched the sky above her.

The young man shoved four Spro plastic topwater frogs into his pockets. He moved with excitement and looked to his left and right to confirm there was no one else around. Scattered beer cans in the bed of his truck laid next to two Shimano baitcaster fishing rods that he scooped into his grasp.

"Abi! Let's go!" he said in a loud whisper. He spoke with a slight southern accent.

Abi walked around the back of the truck with a hesitant smile. "Are you sure this is a good idea, Clay? I heard he shot the last guy who trespassed."

"C'mon, he ain't gonna shoot us for doin' a little fishin'. He might even join us. The pond's only a few minutes walk that way." He pointed the rods toward the heart of the field. He kissed her and smiled. "It'll be fun. There's some monster bass swimmin' around that pond, I'm tellin' ya."

"Okay, we better not be trespassing just for some little dinks."

"That's my girl. I'll race ya there." Clay jumped the fence and took off into the field.

Cows groaned as Clay and Abi ran among them. "It's right up here," Clay said as they ran through the field. The field dipped into a lagoon-shaped pond so that, when standing on the bank, they would not be seen from far away.

Abi stuck out her foot and tripped her boyfriend. "You ain't beating me there!"

Falling face first into the tall grass, he laid on his stomach for a moment and chuckled to himself. Things like that were why he loved Abi, and why they got along so well. She could be as sweet as pecan pie, but would try to beat him at everything as well. Abi was his best friend.

Clay pushed himself up, and Abi had disappeared. "Abi?" He asked, but got no response. On the other side of the lake stood the silhouette of a cowboy sitting on a tall horse with a rifle pointing to the sky. Clay dropped back down to his chest, and attempted to peer through the grass. "Abi!" he whispered, but heard no response. The cowboy rode the horse around the pond until he was less than a hundred feet away. He stopped the horse and got off the saddle, with the rifle resting on his shoulder. He took a few steps, spit on the ground, then got back on the horse and rode away.

Clay popped up out of the grass with no sign of Abi. Still holding the two rods in his hand, he ran toward the lake in a crouched position, knowing the cowboy could return at any second. "Abi!" He stopped at the edge of the drop off circling the pond.

Abi jumped out of the bushes and yelled. He took a hard step backward in surprise. "Jesus, you can't be doin' that shit. You scared me half to death."

She giggled and kissed him on the cheek as she took one of the baitcasters from his hand. "I beat you, by the way."

"I think you were right, that man didn't look like he was playin' around. Maybe we should just go back."

"Oh, now you're gonna siss out on me?" she asked as she pushed through the brush and walked down toward the pond. "We made it all the way out here. We might as well catch something."

"I'm gonna marry that woman one day," Clay said under his breath. He jogged down and nudged her to the side as he took the first cast. His frog landed with a splash just beyond a group of green spatterdock lilies and bobbed up and down on the surface. He held the rod lightly in his fingers, as a golfer would hold a club. He flicked his wrist backward with a quick, short snatch, then reeled in the extra line and did it again. The frog pushed through the water with an aggressive wake after each snatch. Clay plopped it next to the spatterdock and let it sit for just a moment. Just as he was about to twitch the frog again, a bucket mouthed bass exploded on the bait as it skied out of the water. Clay grunted and leaned back against the pull of the fish. "I told ya!" he said to Abi as he reeled in the Largemouth.

She smiled and rolled her eyes as she cast her own frog. Clay gripped the sandpaper-like lip of the bass by his thumb and held out the five pound fish for his girlfriend to see. Its belly had a white sheen and it had a dark green top with black markings and a wide circle shaped mouth. "One to zero." He said and winked at her. "Catchin' fish and lovin' you. Them two things never get old."

Her line became tight as another bass exploded her frog. "One to one!" she said as she pulled in a smaller fish.

"Mine was bigger." Clay nudged her as she pulled in her own bass.

"I bet none of those girls in college can catch a bass like that," she said as she lowered the fish back into the water.

"You're damn right they can't."

He paused and stared deep into her dark blue eyes. It was as if an entire ocean laid deep behind her pupils. "I'm gonna miss you when you have to go back," she said.

He was a junior in college, and it was hard being separated. He had a fun time, especially with his friend Sherman, who loved bass fishing as much as he did, but he missed Abi constantly. "I'm almost finished, then I'll be back with a degree and better than ever. We're gonna be rich." He winked at her. "But we have a few weeks of Christmas break left before I have to leave." He leaned in like he was going to kiss her, but then cast out his frog again. "A few weeks for me to whip your ass in some fishin' that is."

She pushed him. "Jerk."

"There's some damn good fishin' in this here pond ain't there?" Clay and Abi turned around, startled. The cowboy stood looking down on them from the field, rifle resting upon his shoulder.

"Listen, sir, we ain't lookin' for trouble," Clay said.

"Trouble? You ain't tryin' to steal my cattle are ya?"

"No, sir."

"And you ain't vandalizin' anything, are ya?"

"No, sir, just wanted to catch a few bass is all."

The cowboy spit to the side of him. "Well, I don't see no problem with that. You know you could've just asked. You didn't have to go jumpin' barbed wire fences and go hidin' in the grass, like I couldn't see ya or somethin'." He chuckled to himself and shook his head. Clay and Abi's cheeks turned pink with embarrassment.

"We're sorry," Abi said.

"Don't be. Catchin' bass is good for the soul. Way I see it, if more people went fishin' everyday, the world would be a better place."

"Amen," Clay said.

"I always have the best luck in the north side cove over yonder. There's some hydrilla the big'unns get around over there. Y'all have a nice afternoon." He went to walk away, but stopped. "Oh, and make sure you get outta here well before dark. Them coyotes are vicious."

"Yes, sir. Thank you." He waved his hand down like it wasn't a big deal, and rode off on his horse.

Abi leaned her head on Clay's shoulder as they drove in silence with the sun setting behind them. He clenched his right hand in hers and never wanted to let go. All he wanted was to catch bass and be with her. He drove with his knee as he leaned over with his left hand into the side door and grabbed a small bottle of whiskey and took a hearty gulp.

The stars sparkled in the moonlit sky as they pulled up to his dad's house. It was quaint, an old country cottage made out of dade pine, but with plenty of open space around. A black-with-red-sparkle bass boat rested on a

5

trailer behind his dad's truck. It shined in his headlights like it was freshly waxed. An eight foot Power Pole on the back was joined by a two hundred horsepower Mercury motor and a black Minn Kota trolling motor on the bow. Black carpet covered the entirety of the deck. It was a bass-catching machine. "What in the hell?" Clay asked himself as he squinted at the boat.

Abi rubbed her eyes as they got out of the truck. A man of older middle age sat on a rocking chair on the porch. He had a thick, grey beard with patches of brown that reminded him of his younger years. He sipped his beer with a proud smirk spread across his cheeks. "What do ya think?"

"What do I think?" Clay asked. "Whose boat is this?"

Clay didn't think his dad's smile could get any more vibrant, but sure enough it did. "That's ours, son. You ready to go fishin'?"

"Red Booker, you dog! I'm ready to go right now!"

CHAPTER 2

MARIBELLE

Clay's phone alarm sounded in his ear. It would have made for a rude awakening if he were not going fishing. He jumped out of bed, dressed, kissed Abi on the cheek, and was ready for the day.

A single bulb radiated a spotlight surrounded by dark over a teetering kitchen table. The sound of chirping crickets traveled with the cool central Florida winter breeze through an open window in the early morning moonlight. The coffee maker bubbled in the shadows as it spit out the final drops of brew. Clay could smell it in the air—it was going to be a good day.

The end of a black fishing rod leaned on the table as the reel hid in the shadow. His dad concentrated hard on tying a uni knot onto a dangling, lead-weighted hook. A camouflage hat rested above his eyebrows, and his eyes peered with focus through brown rimmed reading glasses. His chin was pointed up ever so slightly, as he looked down at the knot in front of him. With the dark green braided line in his fingertips, he wrapped it into a sturdy knot in a matter of seconds. He pulled the line tight down to the hook with his teeth and gave it a quick jerk to make sure it was a

7

worthy knot. As he cut off the extra line with a pair of scissors, Clay turned the living room light on. A short plastic Christmas tree stood in the corner of the room with fishing hooks and different lures hanging from its branches. A mounted largemouth bass hung on the wall across from Red, with a Christmas hat dangling on its head. Above the bass was a wooden, rectangular sign that said 'BOOKER FAMILY' in burnt letters.

Clay walked into the light with rubber boots stuck into his jeans and shirt that read 'Buoy's Marina, Bait and Tackle'. "Redmond Booker up and ready for the day already. You must be excited."

"Your grandma was the only one that called me Redmond. You either call me 'Dad', or 'Pops', or hell even 'Red'. Anything other than Redmond." He looked up from the knot. "I didn't know we were sleeping in today."

Clay rubbed his bloodshot eyes and looked at the clock over their box television. It was 5:45 in the morning. A hint of alcohol from the night before wafted from his skin as if it were cologne. "I was up late with Abi. It ain't even six yet, Pops, relax. Don't get light for another hour, anyhow. Plus, it's too damn cold to go out right now. Bass ain't gonna eat till it warms up a bit."

Red pulled the hook down onto the pole's hook keeper, slightly above the green speckled baitcaster reel. "Well I want to get out there early. Some weather is movin' in this afternoon." Red looked up at Clay, and his eyes were magnified from the reading glasses. "You're lucky I got everything set up. Now let's go catch 'em!"

"What's goin' on with those glasses?"

"What? They're my readers. I can't tie a knot without 'em."

"You look ridiculous."

Red shrugged, a cup of coffee in one hand and the rod in the other. "Who am I tryin' to impress? You? I don't think so. I can see like a hawk out on the water. That's all that matters, son. C'mon, let's go."

"Alright, let me get a cup of coffee first. We got food and drinks in the boat already?"

"Yep, all packed up, ready to go."

As Clay poured himself a cup, he asked, "You need one?" He turned around, but his dad was already out the front door. "Guess not."

As Clay stepped outside, Red sipped his coffee and leaned his forearms on the side of his boat. The hull sparkled in the flood light. "Ain't she pretty?" Red asked his son in a starstruck voice, like he'd just met the love of his life.

"You did good, Pops. She's a bass catchin' machine." Clay patted Red on the back as he sipped his coffee. "You figure out a name for her?"

"Maribelle."

Clay didn't say anything, and neither did Red. Maribelle was the name of Clay's mother, and Red's wife. One night when Clay was ten, she took off, and they never heard from her again. Red could never let her go, and Clay didn't understand why.

Red shook his head and smiled, "She is pretty, though, ain't she? Let's get this thing in the water."

Red's phone vibrated and rang out loud. "Who in the hell is callin' me at this hour?" He owned and ran Buoy's Marina, Bait and Tackle. Red had opened the marina many years ago. One day, it would be Clay's. Red rarely took a day off. He reached down into his pocket and noted that it was Earl, the man who ran the shop when he wasn't there.

"Hey… No, just order more. No I ain't comin' in today, I told ya I'm going fishin' with Clay… Yeah. Alright, I'll give you a call when we finish. Alright."

"Was that Earl?" Clay asked.

"Yeah, and I ain't dealin' with it today." He rubbed his hands together. "Nothin' like a good cold weather bite. I'm excited." He radiated the energy of a kid on his way to Disney World. "Damn, she's pretty," he said again.

Clay jumped in the passenger seat of his Dad's two door pickup truck, and they took off in search of the mighty largemouth bass. Red turned on the radio, and a fast banjo mixed with static played. "Man, with the water still warm and this cold weather, they should be bitin' good," Red said, almost in a whisper, as he bent over the steering wheel, sipped his coffee, and continued down the empty road. "We're gonna catch some buoys today, son." Red called big bass buoys, because they're so fat and round it looked as if they should float like a buoy.

"Sure hope so. We gotta break her in right on her maiden voyage."

"We will, we will. I'm just glad to be goin' out in my own boat with my boy." Red grinned. "Whether we catch 'em or not. But ohhh, we're gonna catch 'em. Oh yeah, we're gonna catch 'em."

"What're you gonna start with?" Clay asked.

"Might start with a worm, work it slow along the bottom."

"I was thinkin' the same thing. Maybe I'll use one of them crawdad plastics. Why don't we just go out on Lake Okeechobee? Use the ramp at the marina."

"Son, I'm there seven days a week, I don't want to be there on my day off. Plus, the fishin's been slow. I've caught some sea creatures up here."

They headed north from Okeechobee to Kenansville Lake, which was about an hour away. They turned east off of Fellsmere road and onto a long straight dirt path that had a deep and wide canal to the south and woods to the north. It was a fifteen mile dirt road that led straight to the boat ramp. The truck bounced up and down as it plowed over potholes while the static banjo played. Both Clay and Red's bodies swayed back and forth as Red sped down the road at a much quicker pace than most people would drive it. The six rods that laid in the boat bounced like jumping beans as the trailer hurdled the holes. It used to scare Clay as a kid how fast his dad would drive down dirt roads, but he was used to it at this point. Red drove fast wherever he went, but he drove especially quickly if he was on his way to go fishing. No pot holes were going to slow him down today.

Up to this point in Red and Clay's life, they either fished from shore or fished from friends' boats. Anything to get the itch to subside. The itch to feel the unfaltering weight at the end of the line. To smell the freshwater breeze with a hint of fresh vegetation and fish. They could almost feel the heavy lip of the bass on their thumbs.

The road ended at a grass field and a steep ramp that fell into a pocket lined with lily pads on the south side of a 2,500 acre lake. Parts of the lake bordered cattle fields, while others faded into shallow marshland with towering cypress trees and short cypress knees that peeked out just above the water's surface.

The ramp had a dangerously steep angle, and the concrete grip was smooth after years of erosion and trailers backing in and out of it. Tall weeds grew on both sides and through cracks in the concrete. There was no dock with the ramp—you had to beach your boat on the bank for anyone else to get on. One other truck with a trailer sat empty in the parking lot. "Dammit, see, we aren't even the first ones out," Red said as he did a big circle in the lot in order to back the boat down the ramp.

"That's my buddy, Sherman's, truck," Clay said. "I told him about this lake a while ago. He must've been coming to check it out himself."

"Sherman, your buddy from college?"

"Yeah, he's from Alabama. Got a little jon boat."

"You're givin' out our spots, son!" Red said it as a joke, but he would be agitated if Sherman was where he wanted to fish. He turned around backward and reversed the trailer toward the ramp until it was half submerged into the muddy water. He smiled at his son, "Let's go catch 'em."

CHAPTER 3

THE KENANSVILLE CLEAN AND JERK

Every time Clay and Red went fishing, it was as if it were day three of a National Largemouth Series tournament. They were different men when they were fishing. Most people went fishing to decompress, soak up some sun, drink a beer, and if they caught some fish too, then that's great. Not Red and Clay. They went out for one reason and one reason only—to catch largemouth bass.

There was no sitting down to relax or taking breaks. Red only quit fishing to pack tobacco in his lip. They didn't like to stay in a spot for too long. Red was known to pull into a shoreline or a group of reeds, take a quick look around, and if he didn't like the way it looked, he would force whoever he was fishing with to leave without taking a single cast. Most of the time, they believed him. Over the years, Clay learned this fast-paced, all-out kind of fishing from his dad and loved it.

Even when he and Red fished a neighborhood pond, it was time to catch bass, and nothing else mattered. But fishing from shore was a thing of the past, and Red had a shit-eating grin on his face that stretched from ear to ear as he hopped into his brand-new boat. Clay switched into the driver's seat of the truck in order to back the boat trailer into the water.

Red trimmed the motor down and waved Clay to back the trailer further into the water. A single gust of grey smoke puffed from the engine as he cranked it on. It sounded strong and ready to run. Red threw up his hand to signal Clay to stop and reversed the boat off the trailer and into the deep pocket. It wasn't his first time driving a boat—he had been on and around boats since he was a kid. Clay peeled the tires for just a second as he tried to get the truck up the steep ramp, then parked next to Sherman's truck in the grass lot.

As Clay walked toward the beach on the outside of the ramp, he couldn't help but shake his head and smile. With the trolling motor in the water, Red pitched a purple, soft-plastic crawdad into the lily pads next to the ramp. Clay cupped his hands and put them around his mouth. "There ain't anything over there! Come pick me up!" Red turned, half startled, as if he had forgotten about his son. He turned back to what he was doing, ever so slightly pointed the rod at the lily pads, and set the hook. The rod bent into a half circle as a bass rocketed out of the shadows and made a large splash in the calm pocket. Red laughed and looked back at Clay as he reeled him in.

"Well, I'll be damned," Clay said.

Red bent to one knee and pulled the dark green, almost black bass out of the water, holding it by its round, sandpaper-like lips. "What was that?" Red asked as he held the fish up like a trophy. It was a healthy fish, around three pounds. The black markings on its side were abstract, with no real pattern. He pulled out the hook without a problem and tossed it back in the water.

"We could've caught that one from shore!" Clay said as he waited to be picked up. "Come get me!"

Red steered the boat to the shore, and Clay leaped onto the deck to avoid the chilled, late-fall water. As they idled out of the pocket into the main lake, it was still low light, and there wasn't an ounce of wind. A thick layer of fog rose over the lake, and they couldn't see more than a hundred feet in front of them. Water rippled as a dinosaur-like alligator slithered its spiked tail out of a thick brush and away from the boat in the same manner as a snake. A cover of black American coot birds sat in the calm water beside the boat until Red mashed the throttle forward. The coots flapped their wings as fast as they could and began to move their legs in a running motion until they took flight. But just for a second, as they took off, it looked as if they ran on water.

It was dangerous to go this fast in a thick fog, but Red knew the lake well. Cold air pierced Clay's jacket as they raced along, and the wind made his cheeks red. Clay watched his father as he drove. He seemed unphased, his face expressionless, his beard parted in half, waving in the wind as they sped along. It was a smooth ride, and the lake was dead calm. They glided across the water, winding around thick patches of bulrush grass and football sized congregations of lilies. As they slowed close to the west shoreline of the lake, limbs of moss-ridden cypress trees poked out of the fog, but it was too dense to see the entire tree. The boat floated forward as they slowed, and Red turned off the engine. Without wasting a second, he grabbed a rod, and with one long, nimble leap, he was on the bow ready to fish. There was a seat on the deck of the boat, but Red took that off the minute he bought it. He always preached, "You can't catch 'em sitting down. Fish know when you're lazy."

An osprey shot out of the fog above them, and just before it hit the water going at an incredible speed, it opened its claws wide and snatched a bluegill from the surface. In seconds, the bird disappeared back into the fog, grasping its breakfast. "That's a good sign right there, son," Red whispered as he let his hook loose from the rod and ran it through a fat plastic worm. "Osprey and bass eat the same thing." Red tipped the end of his rod down into the water and poked the bottom. "Nice hard bottom, this looks real good." Ripples waved through thin congregations of reed grass from fish pushing across the surface. In front of them was a flat, no deeper than a few feet. Patches of tall grass stuck out of it, taller than the reeds. "Oh they're here." When he said that, he was usually right. Red cast to the left, just outside of a thin group of reeds, and Clay cast to the right, parallel to a thick line of reeds, using the same set up as his dad, except with a plastic crawdad. They both looked around for signs of life as they bounced their soft plastic lures along the shell bottom.

"There he is!" Clay said as he set the hook, and his rod bent over as if he hooked a Marlin.

Not two seconds later, Red hooked up as well. "Yup!" he said as he held the reel up close to his chest and reeled as fast as he could. They both flipped their bass into the boat at the same time and lifted their fish up with their thumbs. Both were healthy fish, just larger than the one Red caught at the boat ramp. Red and Clay bumped knuckles and laughed as they dropped the fish back in the water. Although tasty when fried into little fish nuggets, they never kept their catch. They were pure catch and release fishermen. "That's called the Kenansville clean and jerk right there, son."

"That's a good start right there!" Clay said as he leaned over the boat and rinsed his hands. As he leaned back up, Red was already on the deck, making another cast. That's just how Red rolled—he had forgotten about the last bass and was on to catch the next one. He was always looking around, thinking hard, calculating his next move. He switched baits and techniques until he found that perfect combination that the bass just couldn't resist. He took fishing seriously even though it was just for fun. Unlike Clay, who washed his hands, took a breath, and relived the moment, Red was already out for the next one.

They were both great fishermen. Red had made sure Clay knew how to cast a rod before he could walk. Wherever they wanted to cast their bait, that's where it went. They didn't over cast into the bushes, or miss their spot and have to reel in and try again. They were as masterful with a lure and a fishing rod as a Major League pitcher with a baseball. Bass fishing was a way of life.

As the sun rose above the cypress trees and the air warmed, the fog cleared and it turned into a beautiful day. Red worked the trolling motor as they moved beyond the cypress trees and toward a large patch of tall reeds in the middle of the lake. They were quiet as they underhand pitched their creature baits toward the reeds. They worked the plastic bait for a few moments, then if it wasn't attacked, reeled in and immediately threw to the next spot.

"We'll do a quick circle 'round this thing. I've caught some with Earl here," Red said as he spat into the water. He tossed the creature bait toward a point in the reeds. He twitched the bait once and then threw his rod backward as he set the hook. "Oh, it's a bruiser, son! Work the trollin' motor." Clay pointed the trolling motor toward the fish as it fought against Red. It raced into a thick part of the reeds, so thick that Red would not be able to get the fish out without pulling the hook out of its mouth. "He's in the thick shit, son." He spoke in a gruntled, raspy voice as he fought the fish. "Get the trollin' motor up in it. We're gettin' this bastard out one way or another."

Clay directed the bow of the boat into the reeds as Red dropped to his stomach with the rod clenched in his teeth. He pulled up the extra line until it came tight, and he reached his arm down to his shoulder into the water and pulled out a five pound bass.

"What the hell is this?" a man about Clay's age asked as he stood at the bow of a jon boat that floated around the corner of the tall reeds. He was small and skinny, with a thin mustache and a hat that rested just above his eye brows. Next to him was a tall, plump young man wearing rubber boots and a camouflage hat—the exact opposite body type of his fishing partner. "Y'all think you can just pull up in front of us, then make all this damn ruckus and scare off any fish that're round?"

"Easy, pal. Looks like they were just grabbin' a bass is all," the plump man said to his friend. He scratched his head and smiled. "Mister Clay Booker is who it is! How ya doin' buddy?"

"Sherman! I figured we'd run into ya at some point," Clay said to the big man, and ignored Sherman's friend. "Dad, this is Sherman, my buddy from school I was tellin' ya about."

Sherman's small friend stomped his foot. "I don't care who it is. Y'all need to learn some damn manners! Dumbasses don't even know what you're doin' out here."

"No, they're fine, Dirk. Clay's a friend, and a hell of a fisherman."

"Hey, listen kid." Red said as he dropped the bass back into the water and stood up. "We didn't see ya on the other side, and I sure as hell wasn't gonna let that bass get away just cuz you wanted me to be quiet. Sherman, it's nice to meet you, sir. But you need to go ahead and get your friend Dirk out of here before there's a real problem."

"Yes sir! Dirk, shut the hell up."

"What're you gonna do, old man? Out swim our boat? I don't think so."

"No, but we'll out run your ass back to the boat ramp. You're gonna have to try to leave at some point." Red spit into the water. "And I'll be waitin'." Clay chuckled as Dirk took a scared step back.

"C'mon, Sherman, let's try that group of lilies we passed up north," Dirk said as he sat down and looked in the opposite direction of Red.

"I think that's a good idea," Sherman said. "Sorry y'all!" he said as he fired up his engine and took off.

"What a dick," Clay said.

"Ah." Red turned back toward the reeds and pitched his bait back out. "He's just an asshole kid. Kinda like you."

"Hey, he ain't nothin' like me!"

Red chuckled as he fished. "You got that right."

CHAPTER 4

LEANIN' TREES

They were surrounded by life all day, and no matter where they went on the lake, they found bass. Around lunchtime—and thirty bites later—even Red took a seat to enjoy a sandwich. "Man, we're wreckin' 'em today, Pops," Clay said with a mouthful of bread and turkey.

"It's been a good'un, ain't it? I couldn't be happier with the boat. I was afraid with it bein' new and all, there'd be some kinks we had to work out." He took a big bite of his sandwich. "But nope, everything works like a charm."

"And she catches fish, too. I mean, they're chewin' good today. Anything we've thrown out there today, we've caught 'em on. Worms, crawdads, spinnerbaits, rattle traps, frogs, it don't seem to matter. Long as we can avoid that Dirk character, things are great."

Red nodded in agreement. "He was a little dick, wasn't he." He tossed the end of his sandwich into the water and took a swig of a soda. "Alright, time to get back after it."

"I was surprised you sat down to eat in the first place. You're gettin' soft on me, old man."

He waved off his son's sarcastic comment. "Just soakin' it all in, son. We got it pretty damn good, yenno that?" He sighed and sat back in his seat. "Somethin' about bein' out on the water. Catchin' bass is great, and I can't get enough of it." He laughed to himself. "Trust me. But bein' out here, all my worries, everything else goin' on in life stops at that boat ramp, like there's a big concrete wall where everything bad in life can't get around. If anything ever is goin' wrong in your life, Clay, if for some reason somethin' happens to me, or things are just goin' bad in general, remember the feelin' of being out here. The answer is to fish. The answer is always to fish."

Clay took another bite of his sandwich and nodded.

"Well," Red said as he stood up and tossed his crust over the side of the boat, "I think we've caught enough numbers today. Let's go try to find some studs, why don't we? I want a buoy. And I'm gonna catch 'em with this." He lifted up his favorite lure, a white topwater. Scars ran down the side of the lure, the paint was chipped, and the hooks showed early signs of rust.

"That ol' thing?" Clay shook his head. "Where you thinkin'?"

"Leanin' trees, close by the ramp. Sure would be cool to get a big one on her maiden voyage. We're not gonna catch a lot there—never have—but there's some studs. I guarantee that."

"I don't think I've ever fished that spot before."

Red smiled and hurried to the back of the boat and behind the steering wheel. "You haven't. Probably passed it a thousand times fishin' with other people, though. This is the type of spot you find and don't tell nobody else about. This is the spot we catch that twelve pounder."

"Twelve?" Clay asked and chuckled to himself like he couldn't believe Red thought he could catch a twelve pound bass today, just because he wanted to. "If you catch a twelve today, we gotta stop and get a lotto ticket on the way home."

The main engine roared and spit out smoke as Red turned it on. "Well, if the buoys are anywhere, they're gonna be there."

"Alright, let's go find 'em then."

Clouds moved in from the north, bringing with them a strong breeze and overcast skies. As they crossed the middle of the lake, there was a small chop with the breeze, but the hull took it like a champion. The boat made for a dry and sturdy ride. Red slowed the boat to an idle and turned off the engine as they coasted toward three fallen cypress trees that were holding each other up like logs in a campfire. If one should falter, all three would fall into the water. The limbs reached diagonally to the sky, but the long strands of moss still dangled above the water. Surrounding the three trees like a protective seal was a thick layer of bright green pennywort.

Behind the trees was nothing but a hundred yards of shallow marsh and cypress knees. There was one that stood out from the rest though, a single standing cypress that soared above everything else on the lake. It's trunk was wider than the tallest man, and its roots separated from the base like steep, thin ramps. The limbs were full size trees in themselves, and they held boulders of moss that had accumulated over the years. The tree itself had lived many lifetimes, first looking down upon the Ais Native Americans as they ventured west into central Florida and then Ponce de León and the Spanish explorers in search of fortune. Now it was in the presence of white explorers, looking for nothing but to escape the civilization that they themselves built. The tree was a landmark and could be seen from anywhere on the lake.

Clay frowned as they stood on the deck, and Red worked the trolling motor toward the trees. He looked to the left. The boat ramp was within swimming distance if need be. "Well, I can see why I haven't fished here before." He pointed at the protected pocket to the east. "The damn ramp is right there. I don't see any life. The water's not movin' in here at all. And jeez," Clay stuck the end of his pole in the water and splashed around, "look at how murky the water is."

Red, with the old white topwater lure in his hand, bunched his eyebrows together in seriousness, "Let me tell you somethin', son. The big'uns, that twelve pounder we always talk about catchin', they ain't swimming around with the babies chasin' after everything that moves. Oh no, no, no. They're sitting back in the shadows, waitin' for somethin' to come to them. The buoys, Clay, they lurk in the murk."

Just as he spoke, lightning bolted down from the grey clouds above and clashed with the giant cypress tree. Single strands of Red's grey beard folded upward, and so did the hair on their arms. Chills went up each of their spines as the tree split in half. When each massive side hit the water, it was like an asteroid struck. Water splashed into the sky and came raining down.

"Holy shit! That was a close call," Clay said, wonderstruck, with his mouth and eyes wide open. "Did you feel that? The electricity kinda… go through you? Your beard was raisin' up!"

"Yeah." Red had already dropped his rod to the deck, and looked disappointed as he slouched his shoulder and sighed. "Put your rod down, dumby. Let's get out of here."

"No. C'mon it was one bolt of lightnin'. Let's just take a few casts, then we'll leave. You said there's some big'uns here, right?"

"There sure as hell are. But you know better than that." Red plopped on the seat behind the steering wheel like a child not getting his way. "It can rain on me all day and I don't care, but I don't mess with lightnin'. Especially after a close call like that. Ain't no bass worth dyin' over." Red looked back at the motor as it vibrated in idle.

He put the boat into drive and took off for the short ride to the boat ramp. It began to rain as they slowed down into the protected pocket and saw Sherman frantically cranking his small jon boat onto the trailer. The rain fell even harder, and he was in such a rush, he didn't see Clay and Red as they pulled up onto the beach. Clay jumped onto land and cuffed his hands to his mouth. "Sherman!" he called out. Sherman looked up and waved. "Meet up there!" Clay said, and pointed to the parking lot.

Sherman gave him a thumbs up, finished cranking in his aluminum boat, and ran to the protection of his truck. His tires spun as he mashed it forward on the wet concrete, but they caught grip, and he pulled up the steep ramp and into the grass lot to wait.

Clay ran to his dad's truck and reversed the trailer down the ramp. Red drove the boat right up the middle of the trailer, and Clay hooked the boat up as fast as he could as it poured. Red jumped off the boat and ran to the driver's side door and waved his hands, signaling Clay to move to the passenger side. "Are you serious?" Clay mumbled to himself. "No! Just jump in!" Red ran to the other side of the cabin. He never let anyone else drive his truck, but he was too cold and wet to argue with his son.

"Turn on the heat, son!" Red said as he slammed the passenger door behind him. His beard was soaking wet and fell to a point. He shook his head like a dog, and water splattered throughout the cab.

Clay grimaced and rubbed the water off his face with the back of his hand. "You got me."

Ignoring Clay, Red pointed his closed fist toward his son. "Great first day, buddy."

They hit knuckles. "I gotta agree with you, Pop. We educated some bass today!"

"Wish we could've fished that last spot, but it ain't worth a bolt of lightnin' up the ass. This place ain't goin' nowhere."

"Hell, we should go tomorrow."

Red paused for a minute. "If I can get Earl to cover for me at the shop, I'm in."

Clay chuckled. "I'm gonna pull over to Sherman, he's waiting for us."

"Don't tell me I'm gonna have to whip his little friend's ass," Red said.

Clay rolled his window halfway down as he stopped the truck next to Sherman's. "Hey, buddy! Y'all catch 'em or what?"

Dirk sat in the passenger seat, expressionless, with his sunglasses on. Clay hadn't met him before, nor had Sherman ever mentioned him. "We got into 'em pretty good man! You weren't lyin', this place is great! What about y'all?"

"We wrecked 'em man! Probably got thirty or so!"

"Nice! But the inside of my truck's gettin' soaked! I'll give you a call, I gotta get on that pretty boat behind y'all!"

"Thank you very much! You're more than welcome to hop on tomorrow." Red bent and waved. "If your buddy changes his attitude, he can come as well!"

"Shoot, sounds like a plan!" Sherman began to roll up his window, "I'll call ya!"

25

Clay peeled out, showing off for his friend, and drove onto the long dirt road. "Yenno, I was thinkin," Red said as Clay sped down the puddle-ridden road. "Now that we got a boat—"

"You need to find yourself a woman, is what you need to do. It'd be good for ya."

"We've talked about this, Clay. I ain't dealin' with that right now. Got too much fishin' to do."

"You can't be alone the rest of your life, Pops."

"I ain't alone, I got you."

"Dad, I'm not gonna be around forever. I might move somewhere else. Who knows what could happen after college?"

"I don't want to think about that. What I was gonna say is, you should start fishin' these tournaments. I've taught you everything I know, you could be great, Clay."

"Me?"

"Yeah, you. You have that special touch, son. You can out-fish the best of the best of 'em, I know it."

"I don't know about all that, Pops. Why don't you start fishin' these tournaments?"

"I'm too old to start all that now. I have a business to run. You on the other hand, you have a full life ahead of you, and more experience catchin' big'uns than most do when they're my age. I'm tellin' ya, buddy. Just think about it." Clay nodded in agreement. "And who knows, fish in some local tournaments for a few years, do good., you might find a sponsor or two. Maybe go pro after you graduate." He winked at his son. Red's eyes looked alive, and he grinned at the idea of his son being a pro bass fisherman. He had always wanted to fish in the National Largemouth Series, but never had the opportunity. His time had come and passed, but Clay had a lifetime ahead of him to make it happen.

"Shoot, if I go pro, maybe I'll throw you a sponsor or two," Clay said to his dad and chuckled.

"Well, Buoy Bait and Tackle can be your first. You're a hell of a fisherman, Clay, you could be the best to ever do—" The left tire hit a long pothole filled with water, and Clay lost control. The trailer swerved back and forth in mud, but Clay was going too fast, and there was no way to regain control. The front of the trailer collided with a tall oak tree on the edge of the wide ditch. The trailer was ripped from the hitch as the truck flipped twice and fell upside down into the deep water. It all happened in a matter of seconds. Their beaten faces hung upside down, unconscious, as water rushed into the cabin.

CHAPTER 5

WHEN IT RAINS, IT POURS

Clay stood clean shaven and emotionless at the front of the church entrance as each one of his father's friends greeted him with somber smiles, tight hugs, and words of encouragement that did nothing but make him feel worse. He kept one hand in his pocket and gripped his father's old white topwater lure. Abilene stood next to Clay, tears running down her cheeks. He didn't have anyone else but her now. Her face was ghost white, and, without explanation, she ran to the bathroom. Clay didn't even notice she was gone.

A bluegrass song with heavy banjo and fiddle began in the worship area as people filed into the pews. It was a small church that had three steps leading up to a front porch and two heavy wooden doors that swung open into a worship area with a low ceiling. A gaudy turquoise carpet encompassed the entirety of the room and was rough to the touch. There was a middle aisle and five sets of long benches on both sides. Each bench was occupied by friends of Clay's father. There was a slideshow of old pictures of Red and others that would fade away every fifteen seconds or so as the banjo and fiddle intertwined in a southern duet.

Clay ran his hands through his hair as Abi sat down next to him and put her hand on his, but he moved it away. He could tell she wanted to console him, but he didn't know what to say. He didn't want to talk, and she didn't say a word. With his elbows on his knees, Clay stared at the ground and went over the wreck in his head. He winced, a lingering agony deep in the pit of his stomach sent aches throughout his body. *I killed him. I shouldn't have been driving. He always drove, why did he let me drive? I killed him.* A single tear fell from his eye and landed on the carpet below as the slide show ended and the Pastor began the service. "And Jesus said to her, 'I am the resurrection and the life. Whoever believes in me, though he die, yet shall he live, and everyone who lives and believes in me shall never die…'"

Clay sat in his father's recliner, the black leather of which was cracked in several spots from old age. It had been a week since his father passed. He leaned back as he gulped down the second half of a tallboy. In his drunken stupor, some of the beer missed his mouth and splashed on the chest of his shirt. His eyelids were low as he stared at the television. His lifeless eyes were swollen, with pronounced red veins that took sharp turns and branched into different routes, like a tributary that flowed with red wine. Dark bags separated his eyes from pronounced cheekbones that stuck out after days of refusing to eat. The scruff on his face was uneven and uncared for, like the rest of his appearance. For a boy that was only twenty-one years old, he looked like he had already lived a long and mournful life.

Abilene walked out of the bathroom with her shoulders forward and her head down. She didn't make eye contact with Clay as she sat on the side of the couch that was farthest from Clay. She kept her head down and stared at the carpet, her forearms resting on her stomach. She looked more put together than Clay, but not by much. She seemed in distress and made it obvious. She wanted Clay to ask her what was wrong, but he didn't even seem to notice she entered the room. He got up from the chair, dragged his feet to the refrigerator, popped open another tallboy, and gulped down the first quarter of the beer, then dragged his feet back to the chair.

"I'm pregnant," Abilene said, afraid to look up.

"What?"

"I'm pregnant."

"What? No… no you're not." He laughed, but it was a nervous laugh, like he was in shock. "You can't be."

"I am. I checked three times."

"Three times?" She nodded. "Well damn…" Clay didn't know what to say. They sat there in silence.

Abilene began to sob. "What are we going to do, Clay?"

"I don't know," he said as he stood up, shook his head, and swigged down the rest of his beer. Then he slammed it on the kitchen table. "This is just great," he said, almost laughing in disbelief as he snatched his truck keys.

"Clay wa—"

He slammed the door behind him before Abilene could say anything else.

CHAPTER 6

REDMOND BOOKER

A slow country song with an acoustic guitar and a melancholy tone played over the jukebox in the corner of a smokey bar. The bartender was an older lady with thin, straggly, blonde hair, wrinkled tattoos, and a defeated look on her face that made it seem like she had lived three life-times. Four bikers with black vests and long, grey beards smoked cigarettes and shot billiards in the back while cursing at one another. Clay, now being the sole owner of Buoy Bait and Tackle, decided to close up shop early for a drink or two... or three. Beer dripped down his sparse, patchy beard onto the laminated wood. The beers went down too smoothly as he sat at the bar, and after a few, he was feeling like a champion even though his surroundings told other-wise. It was time for some whiskey.

He coughed as the bartender blew cigarette smoke in his face. She served him a whiskey that was poured in a plastic shot cup. His phone vibrated on the mahogany bar, displaying black letters that read, 'ABI CALLING' with a picture of his pregnant girlfriend in the background. Abi was now eight months into her pregnancy. He crammed the phone deep into his pocket. "Can I get another one of these?" Clay asked the bartender after slugging down the shot. After months of dealing with a pregnant Abi, he was tired of answering her phone calls about nothing.

There was a box television sitting in the back corner of the bar that was as thick as it was wide. It presented a grainy resolution with dull colors. A slow moving fishing show played under the music. It was unnoticed by anyone else in the bar except for Clay. It did not say where the man was, but it was in a freshwater lake, and he was fishing for large-mouth bass. He cast in a slow and deliberate fashion and talked to the camera at the same time he was working his bait, although Clay couldn't hear what he was saying. The old man set the hook and pulled in a big bass that he held up for the camera with a big smile on his face.

He thought of his dad, and pictured him catching that fish instead of the man on television. He would've made it more exciting, that's for sure. He thought of the crash, and cursed himself. It was his fault his father was dead, and it felt like he would never be able to live beyond it. He wouldn't let himself move on. He didn't want to.

A man maybe ten years older than Clay walked through the door in a navy blue suit. He had slicked back hair and pointed boots. He looked like he belonged on Wall Street, not in a dive bar in Okeechobee. He took a seat next to Clay, ordered a martini and turned. "Clay Booker, right?"

"Who's askin'?"

"You're a hard man to get a hold of, Mr. Booker." He ran his hand through his hair, then held it out for a shake. "Hank Monroe with Acreage Bank."

Clay shook the man's hand and turned back toward the bar. "How'd you find me here?"

"It's a small town, Mr. Booker. We've been trying to get a hold of you." Clay sipped his drink and didn't respond. "You're well past due on payments for Buoy's Marina, Bait and Tackle. If you don't do something soon, we will gladly take our property back." Clay took another swig. "Look, you're a young kid, thrown into a tough situation. You're obviously overwhelmed. I recommend selling the place. Take the money and run, yenno? Who needs that dump anyway? We both know it needs more money sunk into it than the entire place is worth. Take the money like your father never could."

"What did you just say?"

"I said your father was foolish for sinking the amount of money that he did into that place. Don't make the same mistakes he did."

"I think it's about time you leave, Hank," Clay said as the bartender placed the martini in front of Hank. "And take your martini with you."

"You have three options, kid. Pay your bills, sell the place, or we take it for ourselves." He took a gulp of the martini and squirmed. "Jesus." He adjusted his tie, slapped Clay on the back, and left.

Clay sighed and ordered another shot as he continued watching the fishing show. One of the bikers leaned on the bar a few stools away. All four men looked mean, but he was especially brutish. He was overweight, with a bald head that sparkled even in the low light of the bar. A tattooed skull on top of his head raged with fire that twisted its way through the eyes and mouth of the skull like jungle vines. The flames traveled down his neck and disappeared behind his leather vest. He smelled like sweat and had a gnarly look on his face. With one eyebrow raised, he cursed to himself as he stared at the bottles behind the bar. Clay's phone vibrated in his pocket again, and again he ignored it.

"Why don't you go ahead and buy me two beers for the next game I beat your ass in!" one of the bikers said to his friend at the bar.

"You better shut your mouth," he said, pointing back. "You'll get what I buy you."

Clay laughed at the television as the bartender gave him the shot, which he downed without hesitation. He wasn't listening to the biker's banter in the least bit.

"What are you laughing at?" the brute asked, now turning his angry expression toward Clay.

"What?" Clay asked, his eyes sagging from the whiskey.

"What the hell is so funny, boy?" The brute cracked his fingers and his thumb as his expression intensified.

Realizing that this beast was now angry at him but not caring, Clay sipped his whiskey casually. "I'll have another when you get a chance," Clay said to the bartender. She glanced up from pouring the biker's beers like he was insane. "Actually you know what? I'll take three more shots. And put it on big boy's tab here." Clay gave him an aggressive pat on the shoulder. "Appreciate it."

The brute looked down slowly at his shoulder where Clay had slapped him, then back at his friends, who were now watching the incident occur. The bartender placed the beers in front of the biker, but said nothing, only stared at Clay like he was a dead man. The brute wiped off his shoulder and began laughing and staring at his friends, who then began laughing as well. He looked back at Clay and laughed at him, so Clay laughed as well. Then, the brute threw his tattooed head forward like a wrecking ball onto the bridge of Clay's nose. A wave of pain echoed through Clay's head, and his ears began to ring before he could comprehend what had happened. He blacked out for what seemed like only seconds, but was harshly awakened as he scraped his face against the gravel outside the bar after they threw him out the front door.

He wanted to yell and cuss them, but the door was already slammed shut. As he went to lift himself up, he became dizzy and spewed blood from his nose onto the gravel below him. He crawled to his knees and sat there for a moment, trying to regain the control of his body. He spit blood onto the gravel as he leaned on one knee. The ringing in his ears was that of a high pitched scream, and dark blotches floated in his vision. He laughed as blood dripped from his nose. He fell onto his back and laughed louder. "What an idiot," he said to himself. "What an idiot." The blood from his nose dripped down his throat. He went to breathe, but the blood clogged his airpipe, and he began to cough. For a moment, he didn't move. The thought of letting himself drown in his own blood felt comforting.

His phone vibrated in his pocket once again. He rolled over and coughed up a pile of blood. He stumbled to his feet, wavered back and forth, and threw his phone as far as he could into the woods across the street.

He mumbled under his breath as he dragged himself back to his truck. He glanced into his rear view mirror, half expecting to see the bikers exiting the bar in a gluttonous rage, thirsty to hand out more punishment. But the bikers never came, and what he saw was a reflection of himself. Both eyes were swollen and had purple and black rings around them that darkened by the second. The bridge of his nose was split open, and a thin stream of blood swirled down the valley between his cheek bone and his nostrils and coagulated onto his facial hair. He reached for a dirty shirt on his passenger seat that he crumbled in a ball and pressed against his nose. He winced in pain before easing off the pressure to the point where it was tolerable. He continued cursing to himself as he peeled out of the gravel parking lot and drove like a bat out of hell back to the house.

Upon arrival at his father's house, Clay realized it was just a house. It was no longer home. It was a nice, older, country-style house, with columns every few feet that drove through the sturdy wood front porch, and dormer windows protruding from the steep shingle roof. He squinted in resentment at the house, still with the shirt pressed against his nose. He stumbled up the steps, expecting to hear an earful from Abi, something he was used to at this point. But as he entered the house, no one was there. He sighed in relief. Abi didn't have a car, but she must've had a friend come pick her up, or maybe her mom. It didn't really matter. As he slammed open the fridge to look for a beer, a note fell off the door, but he paid no attention to it. There was some water on the floor that he stepped in. "The hell is this? Typical. She doesn't even clean up her shit now." He cracked open the beer, fell down onto the recliner, and turned on the sports channel. Before long, he fell into a drunken stupor.

Cold water fell onto his face and into his open mouth like a waterfall, forcing him awake. Clay coughed up the water that was trying to drown him. As he opened his eyes, his vision cleared. Abi's mom, Sue, stood over him with an empty glass and a disgusted look. She was in her mid-fifties. Her short, curly brown hair had gray streaks in it from an extended stint of not going to the salon. "I cannot believe you. You are an absolute pig." She had the same look on her face that the brute did at the bar, and Clay thought he might be in for another beating, but he wasn't sure why. "What, did you get into a fight at the bar?" She laughed and didn't let Clay speak. "Got what you deserved, you drunken slob." She turned and walked into the kitchen where she calmly set the glass in the sink.

"Where's Abi?" Clay asked as he pushed himself to his feet.

"Oh, now all of a sudden you care where my daughter is. She should never speak to you again. You don't deserve her, I think she's finally realizing that. Thank god. I had half a mind to wake you up with a bat to the stomach, but it looks like someone got to you before I could. What a shame. You're lucky Bill didn't come over here, he wants to kill you. I wouldn't let him."

Clay's face was swollen and bruised as he rubbed his pounding head. "Where's Abi?" he asked again.

"She's at the damn hospital, Clay. With your son. Luckily Bill and I were here to get her. You were nowhere to be found. Typical."

"My son?" It was hard for him to concentrate. "What are you talking about? She's not due for another month."

"Well he's premature, Clay. It happens all the time. Not like you care."

Reality hit Clay. He missed his son being born. He rushed to the counter and snatched his keys. "Is she alright? Is he alright?"

"Where do you think you're going?"

"I'm going to see my son," he said as he ran out the front door.

Sue rushed onto the porch behind him. "She doesn't want to see you, Clay! You don't deserve to see him! They won't let you in!"

Clay didn't listen. In a state of pure panic, he sped toward the hospital in the early hours of the morning as sweat dripped from his forehead. He didn't bother to park his truck, he just stopped under the overpass at the entrance to the hospital and ran inside. "Sir, the emergency room is in the west corridor," the woman behind the front counter said.

"I ain't here for the emergency room," he said as he jogged in. "Abilene Douglas. She just gave birth. Where can I find her?"

The woman typed something into her computer. "Second floor, room 5A."

"Thank you," he said, out of breath as he ran to the elevator. He tapped his index finger against his jeans, like a man sending an urgent message in morse code as he waited. As soon as the doors opened, he rushed into the hallway. He looked frantically to the left and then the right. "1A…" he said to himself as he broke into stride down the hallway. He jumped around nurses and patients in the hallway alike. "2A… 3A… 4A…" Clay came to a halt. It was as if time stood still. Through a window, he saw into the room where Abi held their baby. She had the calmest, happiest, most content look on her face as she stared down at their son in her hands. He didn't cry, he only gazed back at his mother with a smile on his face, like he was starstruck at his mother's beauty. Bill sat in a chair in the corner of the room. He had a full head of grey hair and aviator-style seeing glasses. He too was admiring the scene. Bill noticed him, stood up, closed the blinds, and stepped into the hallway, closing the door behind him.

"You have some damn nerve to show up here now. What the hell happened to you anyways? You look like shit. And Jesus, you reek of liquor," he said. "If it wasn't for Abi and Redmond, I would beat your ass right here and right now."

"Look, I'm sorry. I know I messed up. She named him Redmond? We didn't agree on that." Clay tried to step around him, but Bill blocked him. "The hell you think you're doin'?" Clay demanded.

"You're not going in there. She doesn't want to see you."

"I don't care what she wants, I'm goin' to see my son." Clay pushed Bill away and opened the door. He only got a glimpse of Redmond. He and Abi made eye contact, and with no expression, she turned away from him. Bill yanked him by the collar of his shirt and pulled him away as the door shut once again. By that time, the security guard intervened and pushed Clay away. "Get the hell off me!" He yelled as he tried to get around the guard with no success. "Abi! Abi!" he yelled as the guard pushed him down the hallway. "Abi, tell them!"

CHAPTER 7

MOVING TO STAY

Clay pulled into his dad's house with a twelve pack of beer in the passenger seat as he ran over a FOR SALE sign in the front yard. He got out of the truck and tossed the crooked sign in a large dumpster dropped in the front yard. It fell on the old leather recliner that sat on its side atop the trash. Boxes stacked four high sat on the front porch.

Abi walked onto the porch with their baby boy in one hand and a box in another. Her hair was mussed, and she had dark bags under her eyes. "Hey," Clay said as he walked up with the beer in hand.

"Everything is out of the kitchen. Red's room is packed, we just need to pack our room."

Clay kissed his son on his bald head, and Red giggled, his chubby cheeks turning red. "I'm gonna sit down and have a beer or two, then we'll get to it. Have one with me."

"Clay, we have to be out by morning. We don't have time to sit down and drink. We have to take all this to my parents' house tonight."

The walls were barren and plain, pictures were put up, almost everything packed away. He didn't know how to feel about selling his father's house. The house he grew up in.

So many memories of him and his father would be lost, but at the same time, he thought maybe that was a good thing. He felt ashamed he couldn't provide for his family, that he relied on Bill and Sue. Especially after what had happened at the hospital. He was surprised they would even let him in their home.

He dropped the twelve pack on the kitchen counter and cracked one open. He took a long deep swig as Abi walked in behind him, and Red began to cry in her arms. "Can you make him stop, I can't take it right now."

"You're kidding, right?" Abi said over Red's crying as she bobbed him up and down in her arms. "I've packed this entire house, have barely slept since Red was born, and have taken care of him nonstop while you're at the shop, probably drinking by yourself. But you can't take it? Screw you, Clay."

Abi left Clay in the empty kitchen and went to their room with Red. Clay took another swig as he looked around. He wondered what had happened to his life. Everything was going so well before the crash. If it wasn't for him, his father would be here, and he wouldn't have to sell the house to keep the bait shop. He would almost be finished with college, with a degree, and a future. The bait shop was the only thing he had left of his Dad, and he wasn't going to let it go.

He walked into the room where Red had quit crying as Abi soothed him. She looked up at him, then back down to their son. He sat down next to Abi, his shoulders hunched over and didn't say anything, only hugged her. He hugged her tight, his face down on her shoulder. "I'm sorry."

"It's okay, we're going to get through this. It's just a bump in the road is all."

"I've let us down. I missed my son's birth. I can't provide for us, and now we depend on your parents. I let my dad down. This is all my fault."

"You're Red's father. You messed up, but I'm still here. We're still here. We're a family, and we don't give up on each other. It's not your fault we have to sell the house. It's not your fault your dad died. You have to realize that and move on."

"I'm not sure if I want to move on. That feelin' of guilt, it's the only thing I have left of him. I don't know what I want."

CHAPTER 8

A SINKIN' SHIP

SIX YEARS LATER

"Clay, I really don't want to hear about it right now. I'm running late," Abi said as she searched for her restaurant uniform through a pile of clothes in the corner of their room at Bill and Sue's house.

"You're turnin' him into a damn pussy, Abi. I mean, he's in first grade and you treat him like a baby." Red sat on the couch with earphones in as he tapped his tablet. He had a bruised cheek and pink scratches down the side of his face where he fell on concrete. "He needs to stand up for himself. You tellin' him to just talk to the teacher obviously ain't workin'."

"Clay, I talked to the principal. It's getting handled. Have you been drinking?" She snatched the drink from Clay's hand and smelled it. "Jesus Christ." She stormed out of the room and Clay followed. Red looked up from the screen, then back down. She poured the drink down their sink. "How many of those have you had?"

"That was my first one. I promise."

Abi leaned against the sink. "I can't even trust you to stay sober while watching our son. Red—"

"I was just having one damn drink. I'm fine, he's fine. You're scarin' him for Christ's sake. Why don't you just go to work, we don't want you here anyway."

"I'm just tired of this shit, Clay. Please, can I trust you to not drink the rest of the night? My parents will be home soon."

"Not gonna have another sip. Me and Red are gonna watch some baseball, and that'll be it."

"Okay. Okay. Fine, I have to go. I'm closing tonight, so I won't be home until late. Make sure he's in bed by eight thirty."

"Perfect." Clay sat on the couch and turned on the television.

Abi bent over and kissed Red on the cheek. "I love you."

"Love you, too," Red said with his earphones on.

Without making eye contact with Clay, she slammed the front door as she left. It was silent as Clay watched a slow baseball game, and Red stared at his tablet. A burly man stepped up to the plate and, on the first pitch, hit a long home run. Clay shook Red, "Check it out, buddy."

Red winced and looked up for a moment, then back down again. Clay sighed and leaned back on the couch. It was quiet again. He looked out of the front window behind him. Abi was gone. He sighed again and looked at the fridge. Red paid no attention to him, so he got up and opened the fridge. *One beer ain't gonna hurt.* He cracked one open and sipped it on the couch as he continued watching the game. Then he cracked open another, and another, and another. He began to feel warm inside, and talked to the television as if the players could hear him. He didn't have anyone else to talk to.

"We're home!" Sue said as she walked in the door, her purse dangling from her arm, followed by Bill.

"Hey there," Clay said as he sipped his beer.

"Drinking on a Tuesday night, I see," Sue said as she put her purse down in the kitchen.

Clay ignored Sue's sly comment. "Watch baseball with me, buddy. Get off that damn thing."

"But I'm playin' a game."

"Who cares about that game, baseball is on."

"No," he whined, just as any other six-year-old would. "I want to keep playing."

"Fine."

"Doesn't he need to be getting to bed here soon?" Sue asked.

"He's fine." Clay poured himself a tall cup of whiskey as Sue and Bill went to their room. He finished it in silence, and his mind began to race. He didn't want to be stuck inside Bill and Sue's house any longer. Without saying anything to his son, he ripped the earphones from his ears. "Hey, boy. Let's go."

"Where are we going?"

"We're goin' fishin', c'mon."

"But I have school tomorrow."

"See, this is the shit I'm talkin' 'bout. Any other kid would love to go fishin' with his dad, no matter what night it is. C'mon, it's a full moon, them bass are gonna be chewin'. You don't have a choice. Put your jacket on, let's go."

Red hesitated, but put his tablet down and got his jacket from his room. "Mom gets mad when I'm not in bed on time."

"Well, your mom ain't here. This'll be our little secret."

Sue stood in the hallway. "He's not going anywhere with you."

"The hell he isn't. He's my son, and we're leavin' to catch some big'uns. Ain't that right, Red?" Red looked up at his dad, then at his grandma. "C'mon. It'll be fun." Clay grabbed his son's arm and pulled him up from the couch.

"The hell he is, you've been drinking! Bill!"

"I've had a few beers, so what."

Bill came out of the room and grabbed Red's other hand, causing him to begin crying. "C'mon, buddy, let's get you to bed," Bill said.

"Get your hands off my kid!" Clay pushed Bill, who stumbled into Sue, and they both fell onto the hallway floor.

Clay sped out of their front yard and into the moonlit night with his worried son next to him. They rode in silence as Clay drove faster down the road, and it made his son even more nervous than he already was. Clay blinked, imagining his dad in the passenger seat just before the crash, and slowed down.

"I want to go home, Dad."

"Well that ain't gonna happen, son. You need to toughen up. Life is hard, and your mom seems to think coddlin' you's somehow gonna help. Well, let me tell ya somethin', she's turned you into a pussy. And ain't no son of mine gonna be a pussy. Now we're gonna go out and catch some damn bass, and you're gonna like it. I don't want to hear one more word about havin' to go to school tomorrow, or your mom, grandparents, or any damn rules."

Red didn't say anything for a while, and it was silent in the truck. Every now and then, they would hit a hole in the road and bounce in the seats. Clay swerved across the road and into the other lane, then overcorrected and veered off the side and into the grass.

They drove past endless pastures lined with rusty barbed wire connected to wooden posts until they made it to Lake Okeechobee. They followed a road on its coast until they reached Buoy's Marina, Bait and Tackle. Clay pulled into the marina parking lot recklessly and fishtailed the back of his truck on the gravel. When it sat sideways in the middle of the parking lot, he threw the truck into park. "C'mon. We're catchin' 'em tonight." Red's knuckles were white from clutching the door handle the entire trip. He was scared, and he knew there was something wrong. They shouldn't be there. He wanted to be with his mom. He hesitated as his dad got out of the truck. "Hey, boy. What'd I say? Let's go."

One security light shined over the front door of the tackle shop, and everything else hid in the dark. Clay unlocked the front door, ignoring his son, and came back a moment later with a six pack of beer in his hand and lit a cigarette in the side of his mouth. Red followed his dad, who got back in the truck, whipped it around the tackle shop, and backed it up to the barn doors where Clay's dad's boat hid away.

"Open up them doors for me."

"What're we doing?"

"We're going fishin'! Now open up the doors, dammit!"

Red obeyed, opening the doors, and Clay backed his truck up to the boat. Still puffing on his cigarette, he hooked the trailer to the truck. "Are we taking out the boat?"

"Yep, thing's been sitting around way too long. It's a damn shame."

"Doesn't it have cracks in it, from the wreck?"

47

"It's fine." Clay threw the cigarette on the ground and stomped it with his boot. "Couple cracks ain't gonna do nothin'." They got back in the truck, and the rusted trailer squeaked as it moved forward out of the barn and down the ramp. With his hands together, Red rubbed his thumb against his palm in a nervous itch. He sat in the truck as Clay jumped in the boat and turned on the engine, which fired up on the first try. He laughed out loud as he backed the boat off the trailer and into the water. "Red! C'mon son! We ain't got time to waste!"

Leaving the truck, which was still parked on the ramp, Red jumped into the boat and sat next to his dad. They had never taken the boat out—Clay had always told him that it needed to be fixed if they ever wanted to use it. But there they were.

Clay disregarded the no-wake zone and took off from the marina as he opened a beer. They didn't go very far, only a few miles. On the side of the gunnel, sat dusty rods that hadn't been used since the wreck. Clay pulled out two of them and threw one to his son, who stayed seated. Clay stood on the front deck and began casting in front of the boat. "There's a deep ditch out in front of us where them bass will be piled up. Your grandpa showed me this spot a long time ago."

Red sat in the back of the boat with the rod in his hand, watching water trickling in from a crack in the deck and wetting his shoes. "What the hell are you doin'?" Clay asked as he cast.

"I wanna go home."

"Well that ain't an option. I mean, we're fishin' for Christ's sake, this is fun. I got a good feelin' about this spot. Now get up here and start castin'."

48

Red walked through the stream of water that flowed to the back of the boat, afraid to say anything about it, and began fishing. For his age, Red was a good fisherman. Clay had taught him about bass fishing, and they fished off the bank and docks often, just as Clay and his father used to do.

Without a working trolling motor or power poles, Clay let the wind push them down the ditch, but they didn't have any bites. He wouldn't let his son take a break, and they continually cast for an hour to no avail. By eleven at night, Red was tired. "I don't want to fish anymore, Dad."

"I don't care what you want. The world don't revolve around you, son. You're gonna have to learn that one way or another. Keep fishin'. They're around somewhere."

They both used shad-like Gambler big EZ swimbaits and reeled them steadily through the water column on the edge of the drop off. After another cast, Clay set the hook, and the fish on the end of the line didn't budge. "Oh, there he is! Get the net out of the hatch son!" Red scrambled to get the net while Clay fought the fish. "It's a good one! You got the net?"

"Yep, I'm ready."

As Clay pulled the bass up to the boat, Red leaned over with the net. The large bass shined in the moonlight. It looked to be over five pounds. "Net 'em, son!"

Red reached out to capture the fish but missed, and the fish took off into the depths. Suddenly, the line went slack, and the fish was gone. It spit the hook. "Dammit!" Clay said. "How the hell did you miss him? I put him right up to the boat for ya!" In frustration, Clay swung the rod as hard as he could against the deck and broke it in half. Red began to cry. "Oh, that's just great, now you're crying. Go ahead, cry. That'll make things better. Jesus." Clay lit up a cigarette. Red stood in a puddle that had grown to two inches deep in the back of the boat, but it was dark, and Clay couldn't see from the front of the boat. And Red was too still afraid to say anything about it.

The back of the boat was fully under water, and the bow raised higher as more water came in. "Dad."

Clay picked up another rod and cast out. "What?"

"I think there's something wrong."

"Yeah, you need to learn how to net a fish."

"There's a lot of water back here."

"What?" Clay tossed his cigarette in the water and stepped to the back of the boat, and into the ever growing puddle.

"Oh, shit. Shit!" Water rushed in quicker than before. "Get to the bow of the boat, now!"

Red began to cry louder. "This ain't a time to cry, get to the bow!"

Clay tried to turn on the engine, but it only sputtered. "Shit!" He tried again, and again, and again to no avail. "C'mon… c'mon." Red cried on the bow. "Can you quit cryin'? Please?" He turned the key over again, and the motor roared on. He mashed the throttle forward, and Red fell into the cockpit. The bow pointed toward the moon from the weight of the water in the stern. Clay didn't wait for Red to get seated.

With the boat at full speed toward the marina, water began to recede. As long as Clay kept the boat moving, he wouldn't sink. In the time they fished, they had drifted farther from the marina. He didn't pay any attention to his son, who still hadn't found his way to his seat. He stood to try to see over the bow that pointed up to the night sky, but it was an impossible task. He had to look off to the side, and go off his hazy memory.

Red pointed to an old wooden sign that came out of the shadows at the last second. "Dad!"

Clay spun the wheel hard to the right, throwing the little boy out of the boat. He soared through the air, missing the sign by only a few feet. "Red!" Clay said as he stopped the boat and turned it back hard to the left.

He heard gasping in the water in front of him. "Dad!" More water rushed into the boat as he slowed.

"Red?"

"I'm here, right here!"

Clay squinted as he searched through the darkness. "Keep talkin'! I'm gonna find ya!"

"Dad!"

Clay's eyes widened as he spotted his son flailing in the water, then rushed over to him and pulled him out as fast as he could. He ripped Red's jacket off as the boy shivered, and the boat's stern sank. Then gave his son a tight hug. "I am so sorry, buddy. Are you okay?"

He shivered and shook his head. Clay took off his jacket and wrapped it around his son, then looked up to see how close his son was from hitting the sign, and probably drowning. He was feet away from death. "I'm so sorry, Red. But we gotta go or this thing's gonna sink." Red said nothing.

But it was too late. Water gathered quickly at their feet, the bow raising higher and higher once again. He turned the key over, but the motor didn't even sputter. It was dead, filled with water. It was around four feet deep where they sank, and the back of the boat rested on the muddy bottom. They were stuck.

"Shit." Clay mumbled, keeping a hand around Red's shoulder. He stared at his phone. There was no one to call except the police. He knew what that meant for him—he was clearly under the influence. He hesitated to call, but he had no choice. A patrolling marine unit wasn't far from where they sat, and after a thirty minute wait, red and blue blinking lights, along with a spot light shined upon them.

The deputy pulled next to them quickly. "Everybody alright?" he asked as he shined the bright light into their eyes.

"Yes sir." Clay said. "You got a blanket or something on there? My kid fell in the water."

"Let's get him over here. C'mon, bud, you're good." The deputy picked up Red and transferred him into his boat, then got a wool blanket from the console and wrapped him in it. "What were y'all doin' out this late on a school night?" he asked, then spit into the water.

"We were just doin' some full moon bass fishin'."

The deputy spit into the water again. "Is that right? Well, you sure did get yourself into a mess here."

"The trailer is just around the corner, at Buoy's. I think if you give it some ass, we can tow it back."

"You been drinkin' tonight, sir?"

Clay hesitated. "Yes sir, I have."

"And would that have had any impact on why your son is soakin' wet, stranded on a sinkin' boat on a Tuesday night?"

Clay gulped and hung his head. "Yes sir, it probably has somethin' to do with that."

"Huh. That's what I thought. Now I ain't gonna sink my vessel tryin' to tow this thing out of the water. That'll have to wait till mornin'. Get in this damn boat, and call somebody to pick up your kid. Or he's going to child services."

Clay called Abi, who screamed at him through the phone and called him just about every name in the book. He took it without making a single excuse for himself. The deputy handcuffed him after taking a breathalyzer test, and Abi waited at the base of the marine unit's dock as they pulled in.

"Oh, baby, are you okay?" she asked as she embraced her son.

"Yeah, I'm okay."

"Okay, good." She kissed him on the forehead. "Go wait in the car."

Clay stood on the dock in handcuffs with his head down. She slapped him across the face as hard as she could. He didn't say a word or even look her in the eyes.

After a short stint in jail, Clay returned to Bill and Sue's house. His things were packed and waiting for him on the porch. He didn't fight it. He was ashamed. They were better off without him.

CHAPTER 9

BUOYS

THREE YEARS LATER

Heat rays waved through a swarm of no-see-ums. They were so thick that the middle appeared to be solid black. They hovered over a stagnant cove that butted up to the old marina. There were two docks that jutted straight out into deeper water. Both were uneven to walk on, and each leaned to the left after the last hurricane nearly destroyed them. Most of the boards were dry-rotted and needed to be replaced. The nails in them did nothing but separate from the wood so some unlucky boater could stub a toe.

To the left was a single boat ramp with a red and white square next to it that read, '$5 FOR THE DAY'. The right corner of the sign was rusted off, and there were two bullet holes through it. At the base of the two docks, overlooking the marina, was a small wooden shack that was in the same shape as the old docks it overlooked. A single, wide window took up most of the front wall of the shack. A collage of stickers covered the dirty window. There were bass fishing stickers and all brands of different reels, rods, lures, and boats. Some were as old as the shack, having been put on when Clay's father first opened the shop years earlier. A blue neon 'OPEN' sign shone through the dim window above the stickers. The front door was propped open with a stool, and above it was a sun faded sign that read, 'BUOY'S MARINA BAIT AND TACKLE'.

The sun was in the middle of the sky, and the ground was so hot, it seemed like an egg could be fried on it. A small fan, no larger than a man's hand, rested on the edge of a long counter. The head moved back and forth as it circulated the hot air rather than cooling it. Clay sat behind the counter. His thick brown beard touched his chest as he sat with his feet up next to the cash register. The skin on his arms was rough from years of the sun beating down on him. He flipped through a magazine. On the front cover was Dirk Wesley, the friend of Sherman, holding up two largemouth bass. Across the top it read, 'CAN HE EVER BE STOPPED? DIRK WESLEY, THREE TIME NLS CHAMPION'. Clay wore a plain gray, wrinkled shirt, and his eyes were bloodshot, with dark bags hanging under them. With a sigh, he leaned under the counter and took a long, drawn out gulp of a dark, unmarked liquor.

Inside the store, fishing rods stood with the tips close to the ceiling, and there were rows of hooks, soft plastic baits, hard baits, topwaters, and nets. In the corner of the room was a round tub filled with shad live bait. Cobwebs filled with unlucky flies covered each corner of the shack. Unbeknownst to Clay, a mouse dashed across the floor and through a hole in the wall.

A truck pulled in front of the shack, towing a bullet like saltwater flats boat. The bow ended in a point, and it was fully loaded with a trolling motor, twin power poles, and all the electronics a fisherman would ever need. A man and

55

what looked to be his boy got out of the truck. The nine- or ten-year-old boy trailed inches behind his dad as he walked around the boat, studying and mimicking his dad. As the man opened a hatch, his son got up on his toes to see exactly what he was doing. When the dad crossed his arms, so did the boy. Clay took another swig of the dark liquor.

"Howdy!" the man said as Clay jolted out of his seat. The short man was wearing flip-flops, baggy, black swim trunks, and a long-sleeved cotton t-shirt with a redfish chasing a crab on it. The kid had a buff crunched up around his neck like he was ready to go stalk bonefish on the flats of the Bahamas.

"How y'all doin'?" Clay asked, keeping the liquor bottle in his hand below the counter so they couldn't see it.

"Pretty good, bubba, just came down from Homosassa. Little man here wants to catch himself a Lake Okeechobee bass!"

"Well, you came to the right place, then," Clay said with a slight slur. "What're y'all lookin' for?"

The man crossed his arms. "That's the thing. I know it's hot as crap out right now, and we missed the morning bite. What do you think we should do?"

"If I were you, I'd probably just use live shad on a bobber. But if you don't want to do that,"—Clay stepped out from behind the counter and down the middle row in his store—"I'd go flippin' through hydrilla if you can find a good group of 'em. This time of year, them bass like to get under that thick vegetation where it's a little cooler. There's been some big girls snagged these past few weeks flippin'." He snatched two packs of bullet-like tungsten flipping weights, a pack of sparkly purple flipping jigs, some plastic worms, and a pack of beavers. "Use these heavier weights to punch through if the hydrilla gets real thick, and use the lighter ones for flippin' the Kissimmee grass or reeds. Don't go too far back in the stagnant stuff, not many gonna be back there. Stay close to open water where it's movin' a little better." Clay paused for a moment like he was thinking, then walked to the next aisle without any explanation of what he was doing. The man and his son followed behind him. "And if you're havin' trouble flippin'—sometimes it can be hard for kids—" he held a pack of cylinder-like weights connected to two beads on a skinny metal pole, "this can be good too, and it's easy to do. You ever fish a Carolina rig before?"

"Nope."

"So whatcha gonna wanna do here is just tie your braid to the swivel at the end, and then use about three feet of fluorocarbon leader, and use a worm or one of them beavers with a weedless hook."

"And you twitch it? Or what?"

"Not really a twitch. You just wanna do short, slow drags to the side, kinda in the same position you're gonna want to set the hook." Clay mimicked the motion like he had a rod in his hand. "Throw them on points of reed grass or in the middle of ditches or openins into big bodies of water."

"Sounds good to me." He looked around the store. "What else you got?"

"Well…" Clay paused. "We got some bobbers for live bait, big shad bloopers, poppers, topwater twitchers, midwater and deep divers, beavers, big plastics, little plastics, swimbaits, lead weights, tungsten weights, j-hooks, circle hooks, Texas rigs, Carolina rigs of course, splitters, splotters, lines of all kinds, monofilament, fluorocarbon, two pound test to sixty pound test line, braid… let's see what else."

"You said you have live bait?"

"Live shad, yes sir."

"We'll just take four dozen shad then."

"That's probably a good idea. Artificial fishin' this time of year can be hard, especially for the little guy."

"Yeah, you mentioned that."

"Did I?" Clay dipped a net into the tub of shad, then dropped a few dozen of them into the bucket.

As Clay bagged their bass catching goodies, the man noticed a small stack of fliers on the counter. "The Lake O Extravaganza," he read aloud. "Largemouth bass fishing tournament." The front of the flier was a photograph of a Largemouth Bass. Its mouth was as wide as a basketball and it thrashed out of the water with a hook in the side of its mouth. 'OCTOBER 12th' was printed across the bottom.

"A lot of local guides fish it just for fun, but there's all sorta people and boats that fish it. Bass fishin' boats of course, but there's always a few pontoons, gheenoes, flats fishin' boats—heck, last year a guy fished in a bass buggy. It's a sight to see really. There ain't no money in it, but it's good for some braggin' rights. Y'all should fish it. They get some barbeque goin', everyone brings a bunch of food. There'll be plenty of beer for afterwards, it's a good time."

"That does sound fun, maybe me and the boy here will do that. You fish it?"

"Me? No, I don't fish it."

"Good," the man chuckled.

"Why's that?"

"Because you seem like you know what you're talkin' about, and I sure as heck don't. One less man out there that'll beat me."

"Well I don't know about that. But it was good to meet y'all. Go catch 'em up."

"Thanks again," the man said as he and his son walked out of the door and to their truck.

Clay sighed as he watched the boy jump into the boat while the man backed his truck into the dark waters of Lake Okeechobee. Clay wondered what his own son was doing.

Not a minute later, a man wearing khaki shorts, flip-flops, and a long-sleeved, silk bass fishing shirt that failed to cover his large belly walked in. He had a five o'clock shadow, a camouflage hat, and a big smile across his face. "So, this is the place, huh?"

Clay didn't recognize the man at first, but that big belly and bigger grin was a dead giveaway. "What in the… Sherman Puckett?"

Sherman's belly jiggled as he laughed and put his hands out.

"What in the hell are you doin' here?" Clay asked as he hugged his old friend.

"I came to get on some Okeechobee bass, son! Been sayin' forever now that I was gonna make a trip down here. Finally said enough's enough, I'm gettin' down there once and for all."

"You're still livin' in 'bama though, aren't you?"

"Yeah, but I'm down here for a little while! I'm gonna write an article for my website on the big Lake O. Thought while I was down, I'd swing by, see an old friend. Get in with the locals, y'all know the lake better than anyone else."

"It's been what? Ten freakin' years?"

"It's been too long, too damn long, I'll tell you that much. How's the fishin' been?"

"There's a few fish around. But you know how it is. It's still so hot out, hard fishin' after the sun comes up. I was just tellin' that guy and his son there's some big ones bein' caught flippin around the reeds."

"Oh yeah? Nice, nice." Sherman paused as he began to soak in his surroundings. The ceiling had round mold spots from a leak in the roof. The floor had soft spots that felt like someone might step through it at any second. "You been catchin''em?"

"Me?"

"Yeah. You been fishin'?"

"Nah, I'm too busy runnin' stuff here. I don't have any time to go fishin. And if I'm bein' honest with you, Sherman, I haven't really wanted to."

"You don't take your boy fishin'?"

"No… I don't."

"So you just don't fish anymore? Good Lord. What has happened to you, Clay?" Sherman raised his hand over his mouth and pressed his eyebrows together. It was like he had just seen a ghost. "When's the last time you've caught a bass—and don't you lie to me!"

"It's been a while."

He still held his hand over his mouth and lifted it quickly from his face to blurt out, "What's a while?" then covered it once again. He looked like a concerned mother who just got wind of her child cursing for the first time.

Clay sighed, "Three years."

"Three years?"

"It's a long story."

"By God." He crossed his arms and looked away, his grin now a frown, and he shook his head as he stared at the ceiling like he could not bear to look at his old friend's face any longer. "What has happened to you?"

Clay sat back in his chair and didn't respond.

"Well, show me around at least," Sherman said as he snapped out of his disappointed manner. "This place was all you would ever talk about back in the day. You wouldn't shut up about it," he said as he nudged Clay.

"It ain't what it used to be. But I'll show you around. This's the shop, ain't much to see."

Sherman noticed everything that was wrong with the shop—the dirty window, the mold stains, the fermented scent of a decade of dust—but he decided not to mention any of it. Clay had eyes; he could see what was wrong. He didn't need someone else to tell him. "Shoot, I see a nice selection of worms, and split shots, hooks and live bait, what else does a man need?"

Clay grinned and slipped the liquor into his pocket. "I like the way you think."

"Show me around the docks, man! C'mon!"

"Alright, alright. Not much to see out there either." As they stepped outside, the dense, baking air of late summer in Okeechobee consumed them like a sauna.

Sherman rolled up his sleeves and patted his forehead, which was already damp with sweat. "Damn, it's cookin' out here ain't it?"

"That's Okeechobee for ya." The two crooked docks jutted out from the mainland to the right of the boat ramp. From the front of the bait shop, he could see the docks leaning to the left, and Sherman wondered if they were stable enough to hold a heavy man like himself. The first dock came to a stop fifty feet from the land and made a "T" at the end. The second dock was longer and had tall, round pilings of lumber driven into the mud that stood alone from the dock. Prickled weeds grew in thick patches throughout the dirt parking lot and up to the start of the docks, and it seemed like they were the only thing that were prospering.

Most of the wet slips were empty. There was one old cruiser motor yacht on the second dock, which sounded fancier than it actually was. The deck and hull were a matching mustard yellow. There were two levels, with what should have been a white top deck, but it was a dull grey from years of accumulating dirt and soot. Tan curtains covered the windows into the cabin, and scum grew where the water touched the hull of the boat. It didn't look like it had been moved in years, let alone able to get the motor cranked up. "Like I said, not much to see here. That's about it," Clay said with his hands on his hips and sweat dripping off his dark brown beard.

With his lips pressed tightly together and his round chin pushed against his neck, Sherman studied the marina. He was disappointed. He remembered Clay telling him of a thriving marina that was busy everyday with locals, charter guides, and eager tourists ready to catch an Okeechobee largemouth bass. Now, the piece of wood he stepped on was cracked and soft, and it seemed like he could fall through at any moment. As he scanned the marina from the end of the second dock, he spotted a barracks-style barn in the shadows of the tackle shop with its double doors open. Inside, an old boat rested in the shadows with a tarp over the deck. The trailer had two flat tires, and weeds grew like jungle vines through the rims and up and around the axle as they searched for light. "I think there's a lot of work that needs to be done, sure. But there's potential. This place could be sweet. I mean, the location alone, right off a main road, easy to get to. Good fishin' seconds away. Just needs a little TLC is all."

"Yeah…" Clay muttered as they walked down the dock and back to the shop. "Well, that's about it. I don't know how much TLC I'll be givin' her," he said as they stood at the front entrance. In the middle of the parking lot was a brand new, lifted, jet black diesel truck attached to a blacked out trailer and a freshly waxed black bass boat. Painted down the side of the truck and boat was a neon green decal that read *'THE ALABAMA LARGEMOUTH'* in a sharp font with all the letters leaning forward. The boat had twin Power Poles, a 250 horsepower Mercury engine, a self-deploying Minn Kotta trolling motor, and gun metal grey carpet. "That's yours?"

"That's Sheila." Sherman grinned with a devilish expression. "She's a bass catchin' machine."

"Sheila…" Clay shook his head and chuckled. "That's a slight upgrade from the ol' jon boat. The Alabama Largemouth, huh?"

"That's right, brother. That's my website, blog, my social media name, my podcast. I make fishin' videos, too. I've done pretty well with it. But that's my baby right there. She's never seen South Florida water, never caught a Lake Okeechobee bass before. It'd be a shame for you to miss it."

"She is pretty." The boat glimmered in the sunlight. "You goin' out today?"

"I planned on it." Sherman bit his lower lip like a kid begging his parents for a new toy. "Just a quick trip."

"I can't just leave the shop."

"C'mon, you ain't gonna miss any business. Look around." A gust of wind blew dust across the barren parking lot where Sherman's truck and two others were parked.

Clay crossed his arms, and fiddled with the flask in his pocket. "Alright, fine, let's go. Just for a quick ride. But I ain't gonna fish, just watch." He pulled out his keys and locked the front door to the tackle shop. "Let's go before I change my mind." It wasn't that Clay didn't want to fish; it was more that it had been so long that he was afraid too. In his mind, if he started fishing again, in some messed up way, it would be a betrayal to his dad and his son.

CHAPTER 10

FISHIN' AGAIN

"Yee dog! Let's do it." He rubbed his hands together in excitement. Sherman tossed a key with a small neon green bobber connected to it. "Here, back Sheila in the water for me. You think you can still do that? I know it's been a while."

"I'll be fine." Clay jumped in the boat. Sherman backed the trailer into the water, and the engine roared as Clay turned the ignition. He backed the boat off the trailer and next to the dock, and grinned. The slight smell of gasoline filled his nostrils, and he felt powerful as he sat behind the steering wheel, something he hadn't experienced in a long time. There were two large Garmin screens next to the steering wheel, one for a GPS and the other for the depth finder. The depth finder's screen displayed bright colored images as sonar bounced off the bottom. "This is badass."

The dock bounced back and forth with each heavy step Sherman made as he came plowing down. The boat leaned hard to the left as he jumped onto the deck, and for a split second, Clay thought they were going to tip. Sherman's cheeks were rosy red, and sweat dropped from his forehead. "Woo," he said as he dropped down next to Clay. "You go ahead and drive, I need to take a breather. I ain't used to this Florida heat."

"Where we headed?" Clay asked.

Sherman chuckled, and his entire body jiggled. "You're the one who lives here, you tell me."

"Well, I have been hearing some people catchin' fish to the east." Clay scrolled around on the map of the GPS screen. "We'll find some outside reeds to fish 'round there."

Sherman smiled. "Sounds good to me. I got a good feelin', I think we're gonna catch 'em."

"We just mi—" Clay paused. "You might catch somethin'. I ain't fishin'."

"Whatever. Put this thing into drive, see what she can do," Sherman said as they cleared the short no-wake zone. Clay pushed the throttle into drive, and the engine picked up and accelerated faster than he'd anticipated. He slowed down to a manageable speed and sat back as they cruised west. "C'mon, this thing needs to get run hard! It's been a while!" Sherman yelled over the wind.

"Fine!" Clay said as he pushed the throttle farther forward until it was all the way down. The engine screamed as they skipped across the water. They were going so fast, it was as if they levitated just above the surface. They sped through boat trails cut between thick patches of reeds, lily pads and giant bulrush. Even though they were minutes from the boat ramp, the air seemed fresher, cleaner. He gazed out upon the lake, which looked like an ocean. It was calm and seemed to go on forever.

"Now we're talking!" Sherman said as he turned his hat backwards so it wouldn't fly off.

Clay bent behind the short windshield, and wind rushed past him as they flew across the water. His heart raced—in a good way. Adrenaline pumped through him as he ran across the open waters of Lake Okeechobee, which seemed to go on forever. The mild afternoon breeze put a chop in the water, so the boat leaned left and right as it skipped off the waves. Clay eased off the throttle and down to an idle as they approached a long stretch of reeds with some Kissimmee grass mixed in. Clay turned off the motor and propped up his feet as he leaned back. "Well, get to it."

"Alright, I'll go catch 'em by myself, I don't need you." Sherman shook his head and tossed the control for the trolling motor into Clay's lap. "At least work the trolling motor for me while I put a clinic on."

Clay looked at the remote in his hand like it was an alien object. "I don't know how to work this thing."

"It's just like a video game, you'll figure it out. Onward forward captain!" Sherman said as he stood on the casting deck and pointed his rod forward.

"What're you usin'?" Clay asked as he fumbled with the remote.

"What does it matter to you? You ain't fishin'." Sherman under hand flipped a purple and black crawfish with a tungsten weight onto the edge of a thick patch of reeds.

Clay crossed his arms. "No need to be rude."

Sherman didn't answer, only twitched the crawfish back and forth across the reeds. Then he shifted his body weight back as the rod bent over. "There he is!" His voice was raspy from tensing up and speaking at the same time. He reeled down for a minute and pulled the bass out of the water and onto the deck. "Not a bad start right there." He raised the bass out of the water. It was a dark mud green from living in the stagnant summer water, and the black markings were hard to see. It was around two pounds, a fun fish to catch. He showed off the bass to Clay for a moment, shrugged and tossed him back in the water. "First Okeechobee bass! Decent lil' dude."

He fixed the hook back into the worm and flipped it out again. This time, he didn't even have time to twitch it before his line rushed away from the reeds. Sherman reeled up the slack and set the hook on a small one that was pulled out of the water and right onto his thumb. "Two for two," he said as he shrugged again, looked Clay right in the eyes, and dropped the bass in the water.

Clay looked away and crossed his legs as if he didn't care. Sherman wrecked one bass after another. He leaned hard against a bass hooked on the opposite end of his line as it flailed through the grass. "Jumbo bass gumbo!" he said as he picked up the fish by its mouth.

"What does that even mean?" Clay asked.

Sherman shrugged and tossed the fish into the water. Every time he set the hook, he had a different saying. "Ooph!" he grunted as he reeled in. "A little back hand barn door bass action right there." And then a few minutes later another. "Oh yeah! That's a thumper plumper!" He giggled like a child as he lifted a five pounder into the boat. "Mountainous mammoth mouth! Look at that thing!"

Sherman went to flip his bait out again, but Clay stopped him before he let go of the worm. "Alright, alright, I'll try!"

Sherman looked forward and smiled. "The rods are in the port side rod locker." Clay fidgeted around for a moment while Sherman kept fishing. "You still remember how to tie a knot?"

"Funny," Clay said as he grabbed a black and neon green baitcaster. Everything on the boat matched, even the rods. He looped a knot around a crooked Texas-rig hook and pulled it tight with his teeth. As a baseball player would with his bat, Clay jumped onto the deck with his rod on his shoulder. "Might be a little rusty," he said with a tinge in his voice. He was nervous.

"You'll get the hang of it eventually." Sherman spit into the water. "May take a little while judgin' by the way you're letting out that line." They both laughed.

Clay cast the plastic crawdad out, but it was too far and landed in the thick reeds where there were no fish. He had to stop and untangle the bird's nest of line that accumulated on the reel. This happened with fishermen who were inexperienced in using a baitcaster—not men who'd been fishing their whole lives. "Dang it." The next he flipped too short; the one after went to the left of his target, and the one after that to the right. The jig never landed where he wanted. Meanwhile, Sherman hooked two more bass as they made their way down the reed line.

Clay was uncomfortable as he tried to reel in his bad cast once again. As a good fisherman, or just a fisherman in general, one should be able to reel in one's bait quickly and efficiently without stopping to readjust the grip and realign. It appeared as if he had never fished a day in his life. "I feel like an idiot."

Sherman flipped his worm back out. "You look like one too."

"Thanks."

"So, how's things been? I know the fishin's good or I wouldn't have come."

"It's, uhhh…" Clay paused for a moment. "It's alright."

It was silent for a moment. Sometimes, that's the beauty of fishing, the silence, Clay thought. The concentration on catching the next bass with only the sound of heat crickets scattered in the brush and the occasional burst of water from an overzealous fish attacking the surface. Fishing can be a type of active meditation his Dad used to say.

Being on the water let Clay escape all of life's problems and the boat is the temple. It was Clay's place of worship.

Sherman knew that Clay and Abilene had a boy who was named Redmond after Clay's father. He knew that they were separated, but he didn't know much else. Trying to get answers out of Clay proved more difficult than he thought it would be. "How old's little Red now?"

Clay shook his head and cast his worm into open water. He hadn't gotten a single bite.

"Clay," Sherman said again.

"Huh?"

"How's Red?"

"Oh, he's uh… he's alright I guess."

Sherman pushed his eyebrows together as he cast again. "Just alright?"

"Well he stays with his mom most of the time… well, all of the time." Clay turned and flipped his worm next to a group of reeds and sighed. "If I'm bein' honest with ya Sherman, I don't really know how he's doin'. It's been a while since I've seen him."

"How long is a while?"

Clay gulped, his cheeks turning red from shame. "Since we went fishin' last, three years ago. I send him money and a note for his birthday and Christmas, and that's that." He swallowed again as he tried to clear the knot in his throat. Sherman couldn't see due to Clay's sunglasses, but his eyes were swelling with tears. "It's best that way."

"Clay, that's horrible. What are you talkin' about? How is it best that way? Red needs his dad, just like I needed mine and you needed yours."

"Yeah, well, mine's dead. I killed him."

Sherman quit fishing for the first time the entire conversation and almost whacked Clay with his fishing rod as he turned with his hands on his wide hips. "You got into an accident. You didn't kill him. And you might as well be dead to Redmond. What the hell is a note good for, Clay? Now I don't care what has happened in the past. The past is the past and there's nothing we can do about it. Your dad died, and that really sucked. That really, really sucked. But that was ten freakin' years ago. You're putting your kid through the same thing you had to go through with your mom leavin' you. You need to man up my friend because you have a kid that needs you more than ever. And to be honest, you need him too. I love ya buddy, but you look like hell. Don't think I didn't notice that flask in your pocket either."

Clay wiped his nose in embarrassment and looked away from Sherman, who was eyeing him down just as a hawk would eye its prey. Clay didn't know how to respond. What could he say? Sherman was right. "You don't get it. Abi won't let me see him."

"She has to let you see him. What the hell did you do?"

"It wasn't one thing, just a whole bunch of mistakes that just kept on snowballin' until she'd had enough. She said I wasn't fit to be around our child." A single tear ran down his cheek.

"That's tough buddy. I'm sorry to hear that. But you can't just never see him again. Get your shit together and do whatever it takes to be in that kid's life. Even if it starts out as just an hour a week, don't matter."

"You're right," Clay said as he flung his bait out.

"You need to get him out on the water. I bet Big Red would be happy to see you two fishin' together."

"Yeah, he definitely would." Clay smiled. "Shoot, I'm happy to be fishin' again. Feels good to be out here, even if I do look like I never fished a day in my life." Just then he paused and held his entire body still. His line moved just a hint away from the reeds. "There he is…" he whispered, then set the hook. The fish stayed down and pushed for the reeds. "Oh, it's a good one!" Clay reeled and pulled the bass toward the boat.

Sherman leaped down from the front deck and pulled out the net. "Just pull him over, real easy!" he said as he leaned over the side of the boat with the net. The bass skied out of the water like a blue whale as it flared its mouth back and forth, trying to shake the hook with no success. "Easy!" he said again, teeth clenched. Clay reeled one last time, then pulled the bass right into the net. "Atta boy!" Sherman said as he raised the fish out of the water.

"Woo! Nice! That's a good'un'!" Clay said, out of breath. He squatted down and picked up his first bass in years. Its mouth was as wide as a hand, and its belly was fat and swollen. There was a twinkle in Clay's eye as he examined the fish up and down.

"Oh, look at that thing! Let's see how much she weighs! I'm thinkin' six, maybe seven."

"Yeah, I'm thinkin' about the same," Clay said, eyes wide.

Sherman put the dull hook connected to the digital scale under the bass's jaw and let it hang. "Six point three pounds! Atta boy! What a start!" They high fived, and Sherman took a quick picture on his phone. Clay unhooked the scale and placed the fish back in the water. He let it breathe for a minute, and then it swam back to where it came from. "How the heck did that feel? First bass in years, and it's a stud! You still got it."

"Man, I can't lie, that felt good!" They laughed and shook hands. "Now that's a buoy!"

"A buoy? What do you mean?"

"Buoy is a big ol' fat bass. That's what my dad started callin' 'em years ago."

"A buoy... hmm, I like that."

Just like that, Clay was hooked again. They ended up fishing the rest of the day, and Clay's casts became more accurate, his motion smoother. They caught a good number of fish despite the blazing hot end-of-summer day. Catching a six pounder constituted a great day of fishing at any time of the year. Clay was glad to see Sherman, and his boat was great to fish on, but he couldn't help thinking about his dad's old boat that sat behind the shop, rusting away. He imagined himself and his son fishing on it, and he smiled.

They ran back toward the marina as the sun set to the west. Clay rediscovered the feeling that comes with fishing—the feeling of being away from the world's problems and forgetting about them, if only for a second. The wind blew his beard into two even sections around his neck as the late afternoon sun sat low in the sky. Lightning struck far out in the distance under the grey afternoon storm clouds, which were outlined with wild arrangements of orange and pink rays from the setting sun. He thought about his son and wondered how he was doing. He hoped Red was happy.

As they pulled back into the marina, Clay helped Sherman put Sheila back on the trailer, and they made plans to fish again. "I hope you don't think I was bein' hard on you back there," Sherman said as he opened the door to his lifted truck. "Just wanna see what's best for you, buddy, that's all."

"I know it. It's just been so long at this point, don't really know what I'm gonna do."

"Just try, that's all you can do." Sherman patted him on the shoulder. "I gotta get some editin' done for my next video. I'll give you a ring tomorrow." He climbed up the steps to his seat. It was impressive to see a man of his size get up those steps, and Clay wondered how he did it every time. Sherman sped off toward his hotel, leaving Clay in a cloud of dust and black smoke.

And just like that, Clay was alone again. It was nice to have someone around. He spent most of his days alone at the marina, with the occasional customer here and there. He unlocked the front door to the shop, and as he flicked on the lights, a roach darted across the floor. He smiled, but it wasn't a happy smile or a smile of contentment. It was the smile of a man trying to trick himself into being happy, but for whatever reason, it only made him feel worse.

He walked to the back of the store until he reached another door that appeared to lead to a closet. Instead, it was a small room with a fold out couch, a miniature fridge, a desk, and a sink with a toilet. On the table were miscellaneous papers, mostly bills that were all marked 'LATE'. It was a single step above a jail cell. The bed squeaked as he plopped down on it, and reality set in. He pulled out the flask from his pocket and twisted off the cap.

CHAPTER 11

BACK TO REALITY

Clay stared into the dark abyss that was his flask full of liquor. He swished the tin container back and forth. Next to his bed was a printed picture of him holding Redmond for the first time, a few weeks after he was born. He sighed and looked back down at his flask, then started to take a sip but stopped himself. He stood up and poured it down the sink. He remained there for a minute, leaning on the sink, head down as the remaining sips fell down the drain. A part of him wanted to clog the hole and lick up the little alcohol left in the sink. He looked over at the stack of bills from the bank that weren't going to get paid anytime soon. That wasn't something he could deal with right now, so he left his cell and walked around back to the barrack style barn.

The doors were open—he kept them that way. Around those parts, he didn't have to worry about anyone stealing. Dust covered just about everything in the barn. The perimeter was covered with old tools, sports equipment, and fishing gear that would be considered antique. In the middle was a boat, and he rubbed his hand on the tarp as he walked down the side. A cloud of dust rose into the air as he ripped it off. Clay coughed and waved his hand back and forth as he tried to escape the airborne dirt. The dust settled through the rays of afternoon light that found their way through cracks in the metal walls. It had been three years since the boat had been moved, and that had been the only time in the last ten years. Even after all that time, there was still a dull red sparkle shining from the hull, like an old dying star in the far distance of the universe. A slight smile slid across his face. With the bottom of his palm, he rubbed the dust off the motor's two hundred horsepower sticker. He whistled through his teeth like he was impressed. "Thing's still bad," he whispered to himself. Cobwebs filled all corners of the boat, and there was a small hole through the carpet and into the front hatch from rats. The front windshield was no longer transparent after years of buildup, and the dash with the electronics was covered in rat droppings.

He took one slow step at a time toward the bow, small puffs of dust blowing into the air as he exhaled. Rust ate away at the metal handles and parts of the trolling motor. He stopped a few feet from the bow where a long crack began. He put his hand on the crack and continued walking to the bow where one turned into several lightning-like splits in the hull, all leading to one blunt force blow at the very end. As Clay blinked, he saw flashbacks of himself and his dad swerving back and forth on the dirt road. The end of the boat slammed into the tree and sent the truck flying into the ditch, all in a matter of seconds. He lifted his hand off the cracked hull and came back to reality. A tear ran down his cheek.

He jumped into the boat, sat behind the steering wheel, and gripped it as if he were about to drive it off the trailer right then and there. Mold grew on the carpet in the back of the boat from water damage, and he thought about Redmond and the last time the boat was used.

"What're you doin', man?" Startled, Clay looked up to see Sherman with a six pack of beer in his hand. "I've been wanderin' around the marina for ten minutes tryin' to find—" Sherman quit what he was saying and stood with his eyes wide open. "That's your dad's, ain't it? I noticed it before, but I didn't realize. This thing ain't in bad shape, buddy." Sherman whistled just as Clay had when he made his way down to the Mercury motor. "I still think this is the best motor they ever made. I bet we could get this thing runnin' in no time."

"Back already? You miss me that much?"

Sherman cracked open a beer with his teeth and spit out the cap. "Yeah, figured you might like some company. But I'll tell you what, after one look at this thing," he stared at the boat with a fierce intensity as he sipped his beer, "you need to get this boat on the water, man. This thing is brand spankin' new. There's a few cosmetic issues, sure. But all things considered, ain't bad." He sipped his beer again. "Ain't bad at all."

"I was just thinkin' that. I'd like to get Red in here with me, get this thing runnin' again."

Sherman snapped his fingers and pointed toward his friend. "Booyah. Took the words out of my mouth."

"Hell if his mom would ever let that happen, though."

"You want a beer?"

Clay clenched his jaw and ground his teeth back and forth. He really wanted to say yes. "No, I'm alright."

He smiled. "I hope you don't mind if I polish these bad boys off myself, then."

"Be my guest."

"But I gotta tell ya, when we were standing out on the dock today, I saw this thing sitting in the shadows. And I couldn't stop thinkin' about it. I only saw it for a second

77

while you were showin' me around, but somethin' told me to come back," he said in a serious, almost spiritual way. "And I also didn't want to drink beer alone. But it looks like that's probably gonna happen."

"I need to get my son back, Sherman."

Sherman crossed his arms, sipped his beer again, and nodded.

"But what am I supposed to do? Just show up to Abilene's place—'Hey! It's me. The deadbeat dad. Let's redo this boat together, son.'"

"That might work."

"She'd probably try to shoot me."

"I don't know what you should do, but what I do know is you shouldn't put this off one more day, my friend."

CHAPTER 12

GOIN' TO CHURCH

Clay woke up at five in the morning, his back aching from the uneven bed and his mind racing. He'd had a hard time falling asleep—his brain wouldn't stop thinking about today. He went over the scenario in his head a thousand times, and he still didn't know what he was going to say to them. What could he say?

He'd thought about calling the previous night to let them know he planned on coming over, but there was no use to that. On the off chance that she would even pick up his phone call, there was no way she'd let him come over. Better to just show up and hope for the best. The nighttime crickets chirped their final verse as Clay stepped into his outside shower. A brown frog with big yellow eyes stared at Clay like he was some sort of monster, then hopped out of the shower as he swatted the creature away. He was nervous and stood there until the water grew cold, thinking of what he was going to say. It was fruitless; he came up with nothing worthwhile. There was nothing he could say to mend things immediately like he hoped, but he wasn't that foolish. Something like this was going to take time. It was going to be a slow process that he wasn't sure would even work. Abi needed to be on board with Clay coming back into Red's life, and most importantly, he needed Red to want him back in his life. He wasn't sure he could convince either of them.

It was six in the morning when he sat down at his uneven wooden desk, the top of which featured circular condensation stains from past drinks. A pile of unopened envelopes was stacked in the corner. Most were junk mail, but some were from Acreage Bank. The money from selling his father's house had only delayed the inevitable, and it was all but gone now. He had been putting off opening them. He already knew what they were—past due bills. The last year had been slower than normal, and many people went elsewhere for fishing supplies. He sighed as he opened the letter from the bank labeled 'IMPORTANT' in big red letters. His fingers shook as he opened it, now facing the truth he had been delaying. It had been over four months since his last payment, and he knew he didn't have the money to pay it now. He began to tear off the top, then stopped and tossed the envelope back onto the table. "Shit…"

Instead of putting himself in a bad mood, he decided he'd get a little work done on the docks. He hadn't worked on them in a while, and they needed love. He sat in his chair and made eye contact with a shot or two floating at the bottom of an old bottle he had forgotten was there. He could finish the bottle, go to the liquor store, and forget about this whole thing. His mouth salivated like one of Pavlov's dogs. His dad would have back handed him across the face for even considering what he was thinking. The bottle shattered into a hundred pieces as he threw it against the wall, then left the room without cleaning it up.

With a hammer and cup full of nails in his hands, he ventured out of the bait shop and onto the docks. The sun was just rising, and he figured he had an hour before he would go over to their place. They'd be going to church, and he could catch them in a good mood beforehand, maybe take Red to breakfast instead.

Clay hammered each piece of loose wood with a nail, and any old nail that had pushed its way upward was re-placed with a new one. Even though it was early in the morning, the humidity felt like a heavy blanket resting on his shoulders, and it made each breath a struggle. It wasn't long before he was covered in sweat and dirt. By the time the sun came up, he had gotten lost in his work, and realized too late that it was ten minutes past time to leave.

They lived in the adjacent town, and he wanted to catch them before they left for service. "Dammit," he said as he looked at his watch. It was seven fifteen. He wore a white shirt with dirt streaks on it, and sweat dripped down his arms. He didn't have time to change, so he ran to his truck, which took two tries before it cranked up, and sped out of the empty dirt parking lot.

Abi and Red lived with Abi's parents in a mobile home on a small piece of land with a cow pasture as their back-yard. It was not fancy by any means, but they kept their yard manicured, with short green grass and pink flowers lining the front of the porch and a concrete walkway. As he parked his truck, Abi and Red walked out of the front door with their Sunday attire on. Abi was in a rush and looked flus-tered as she led Red out of the house by his hand. She wore a long, light yellow dress with white flowers on it. Red's hair was parted to the side, and he wore a collared shirt with slacks and a belt. She was in such a hurry she didn't notice

Clay's truck until she turned around to walk to her car. When she spotted him, she stopped in her tracks. He couldn't take his eyes off his son. Red had grown so much in the last three years. He was coming up on his tenth birthday soon. A tear fell from Clay's eye as he smiled at his son.

Abi made eye contact with Clay, and then he focused on her. He got out of his truck, embarrassed at how he looked while they were so put together. Abi turned to Red and shooed him back into the house, shutting the front door behind him. Clay's heart pounded as he walked up the path and stopped at the stairs that led to the porch. Abi had her arms crossed and a stern look on her face. "Hey," he said.

"What are you doing here?" she asked, looking down on him.

"I, uh…" He paused, and a fit of agitated anger ran through him. She knew what he was doing there. "I'm here to see my son—"

"Oh, that's it? Just show up at seven thirty in the morning after three years?" She looked up to the sky. "I can't believe this, really. Right before church, too."

"Yes, right before church. Somethin' needs to change. I need to be with him. I'm not askin' for a lot. Maybe I could just take him to breakfast."

"What, are you drunk? You look like you've been up all night drinking."

Sue and Red peaked through the front window and watched them talk. A man Clay didn't recognize cracked open the front door. "Is everything okay, honey?"

"Honey?" Clay asked.

"I'm fine," she whispered to him. "I'll be inside in a minute."

"Okay." He closed the door.

"Who in the hell is that?"

"That's my boyfriend, Hank. He's none of your business."

"Of course he's my business. He's around my son, he's my business." He shook his head. "Look, I didn't come here to fight. I just wanted to see my kid. I've been workin' all morning. I know I haven't been there for you and Red, but I want that to change. I don't know what to say, except that I'm sorry, and that I want to do better. I need to be in Red's life."

"What a joke." Abi rolled her eyes and laughed. "Get off my property," she said as she turned around and was greeted by her Mom.

Sue whispered something to Abi. They began to bicker back and forth, but Clay couldn't hear what they were saying. "No… most definitely not," Abi said to her mom. By this time, Bill had stepped into the doorway, glanced at Clay, and intervened in the quarrel. They murmured back and forth for another minute, then Abi stormed back in the house. Sue followed and closed the door behind them.

Bill, with his hands in his pockets, took his time as he walked down the steps. "Clay," he said as he greeted him with a hand shake.

"Bill."

"You've been a real piece of shit to my daughter and my grandson."

Clay looked down at his feet. A lecture by Bill was the last thing he wanted. "You don't have to tell me who I am, Bill. I know what I've done."

"But I think everyone can change, and I hope that's why you're here. I've done a lot of things in my life that I ain't too proud of either. All I'm saying is, no one can stop you from going to church. We may not want you there, but we also can't stop you from coming."

Abi walked back out of the house with Red by her side, followed by the man who had stuck his head out of the door. She guided Red with her hand on his back as they walked down the steps. Clay and Hank stared at each other as Hank walked toward his car. "Hey, buddy," Clay said as he smiled at his son. Red had turned into a little man. He looked at his father with a shy smile.

"C'mon, Redmond. We're gonna be late," Hank said and patted Red on the back. And that's when Clay realized who he was. The man in the suit from Acreage Bank who found him in the bar. The man who insulted and threatened him. The reason he had to sell his father's home.

Sue wobbled down the steps with her high heels on and stood behind her husband. "Come to service, Clay. You need a little Jesus in you," she said.

"Oh, I don't think so. Church ain't really the place for me. Abi don't want me there, and I don't want to ruin y'all's Sunday."

"You do whatever you want, Clay. God knows you have up to this point. But you came here wanting to see your son. Now you have an opportunity to. Abi isn't going to want you around at all, and for good reason. Show her you're serious about making a change," Bill said, face like a stone. "Because right now, she thinks this is just another fling. And to be honest so do I. You haven't been here for your son, Clay. You can't expect to just waltz back into his life like nothing has happened. That's something you're going to have to earn."

Clay sat in his truck as he watched Red, Abi, and Hank drive away. *Just go home, they don't want you. They're better off without you.* He threw his truck into drive and peeled out back toward his shop. As he drove in silence, he thought about how disappointed his father would be in him. Clay remembered how devastated he was when his mom left them. There was a void in his life because of her. Here he was, quitting on his family once again. That's why there was another man in their life, and that's why he hadn't seen his son in three years—because he was a quitter. A loser who couldn't get over an accident that had happened ten years ago. And he was finished. He wasn't going to quit any longer. He slammed on his breaks and made an aggressive U-turn in the middle of the road, back toward the church.

As he pulled into the church's parking lot, shivers crawled down his spine. It was the same church where his father's funeral was held all those years ago. He gripped the steering wheel with white knuckles as he watched the late stragglers rush into the open doors where the pastor greeted the congregation. Clay watched from his truck as Bill and Sue walked through the doors, and his first instinct was to leave. This was no place for people like him. His beard was uneven, he wore torn up jeans, and he was covered in dried sweat and dirt. "Dammit." He put the truck in park and hurried to the open doors.

The pastor gave him an odd look but smiled anyways. "Hello, I'm Pastor Dave. Nice to meet you."

They shook hands. "Clay, nice to meet you."

He closed the door behind Clay since it was time for the service. But the Pastor didn't make his way to the front as he would during any other service. Instead, he patted Clay on the back. "Good to have you here."

"Well, thanks. Good to be here."

"You own Buoy Bait and Tackle, correct?"

"Yes sir, I do."

"I've used your marina in the past," he said. "Well, at least I used to. I sold my boat. Fighting the devil is a full time job with a whole lot of overtime."

"Yeah, well, you're right about that." The pastor looked intently at Clay, but Clay looked into the congregation, where everyone watched with judgmental eyes as the pastor talked to some bum. Abi rolled her eyes and whispered into Hank's ear; Red peered over the back of the bench with a smile, amused that it was his father holding up service.

"How's the fishing been lately? Probably decent in the morning and that's about it, huh? Man, I need to get out there. God meant for us to be out on the water, yenno. That's why the Earth is covered in it. There's something spiritual about it."

"That makes sense. I don't wanna be rude, but don't you got a service to run?"

The pastor seemed enthused to talk fishing with Clay, and less enthused to talk God. "Ehh…" He turned toward the group of Christ-loving, judgmental eyes watching his every move. "Yeah, I guess. Find a seat wherever, my friend. Can't keep the people waiting, they'll get restless… We'll continue this conversation later." Clay squeezed into a spot at the end of a bench in the back of the room. The elderly lady he sat next to gave him a disgusted glance under a towering white floppy hat with flowers attached to it. The message that she thought it was preposterous that he would dare come to church in his sullied attire was clear. Pastor Dave clapped his hands once, and it echoed throughout the room as he strutted down the middle of the aisle and began the sermon. Clay didn't hear a word Dave preached; he was too distracted by his son, who seemed happy to be there. His hair had darkened from a sandy blonde to brown, just like

Clay's, and although he looked a lot like Abi, Red resembled his father as well. The boy swayed back and forth as gospel music played, and, every once in a while, peered back at Clay, who gave an inconspicuous wave and pointed to the pastor as if to tell him to pay attention. Abi caught Red with his attention on his dad. She turned his shoulders toward the front as if to say, *don't pay attention to that man back there, he'll leave again soon.*

As the sermon ended, Abi did not linger. She pushed past her parents unapologetically. Dragging Red by the hand, she was the first one out of the church and through the front doors, followed closely by Hank. Held up by Pastor Dave, who wanted to talk to him about what color flipping jigs he preferred, Clay watched her run out the door. "Pastor, I prefer usin' dark colors. Now, I'm sorry, but I gotta get goin'."

"Alright!" he said as Clay broke into a run down the short hallway and out the door. "We'll talk more next week!"

Clay burst outside. Abi shut the back door to her car, where Red sat looking out at his dad. She glanced at Clay as she got into the driver's seat. "Abi!" he yelled as he ran through the parking lot. She tried her best to back out and take off as fast as she could, but he ran in front of the hood, and she came to a screeching halt. Red clenched his seatbelt in fear.

Abi rolled her window down an inch. "Get out of the way, Clay!"

"Can I talk to you—to Red and you? Just for a minute. Please."

"Oh, now you want to talk?" she yelled through the cracked window.

"Why don't you just leave, buddy? Like you did before? They're better off without you," Hank said.

Clay looked at Abi. "I know he didn't just say that to me. If my son weren't in the back seat, I'd have 'em spittin' blood already."

"He's right, Clay. You think you can just show up one day out of nowhere and expect me to be alright with that? Expect Red to be alright with that?"

"I haven't been the best dad, but that don't mean—"

"Haven't been the best dad? You haven't been a dad at all, Clay! One day at church isn't going to change that!"

"He's about to be a business-less loser as well," Hank said.

"Goodbye!" She mashed on the gas and almost ran over Clay. Maybe she was trying to, but he jumped out of the way. Red stared at his dad through the back window as they drove off.

Clay held his hand up, but felt defeated, and more like a bum than he did beforehand. "Shit..." he said, out of breath. The entire congregation stood at the front door with crossed arms and raised eyebrows. "What're y'all lookin' at?" he asked from across the parking lot. The silent crowd dispersed like nothing had happened. Clay rolled his eyes and stomped back toward his truck.

"Clay! Clay!" Bill walked with his hand in the air as if he were calling a cab on the side of the street in New York. Sue followed behind him, taking small, quick steps in her high heels, her knitted purse dangling from her forearm.

Clay closed the door to his truck and manually rolled down the window as the Douglases rushed forward. *Here we go again*, he thought. Sweaty, well under dressed, flustered, and embarrassed, he sat there with blushing cheeks, waiting for Bill to tell him once again what a horrible person he was.

"Appreciate you waiting," Bill said as he patted his wrinkled forehead with a handkerchief, out of breath.

"No problem," Clay said and sighed.

"We saw what just happened."

"The whole congregation saw it!" Sue said as she caught up.

"Yeah, sorry about that. I didn't mean to make a big ordeal out of the whole thing."

"Look, I don't know what you've been up to lately, obviously. And personally, I don't care. Abi is doing just fine on her own with a little help from us and Hank. But if you really want to be a part of Redmond's life, you need to show Abi that you've changed for good. I don't think there's much you can do right now, but come to church again next week. Show Abi that you really care, because if I'm being honest, right now she thinks you're full of shit—"

"William!" Sue slapped his shoulder with her purse.

"You think they'll let me back in after all this?"

"Well, some of the ladies probably won't be too happy about it, but I think if you're on your best behavior next week, they'll get over it. And Pastor Dave told me to get you to come back. He needs someone to talk fishing with."

CHAPTER 13

FIRST THINGS FIRST

The next morning, Clay rolled out of bed, and for the second day in a row, wasn't hungover—something he wasn't accustomed to. It was a horrible feeling indeed. His stomach twisted in a sharp pain that forced him to sit back down. Sweat dripped from his forehead even though he shivered. His body had grown accustomed to the liquor. *One drink and this could all be over.*

After a long shower, he flipped on the lights to the shop and frowned as he studied his business with sober eyes. His face was pale, bags hung under his eyes, he knew that if he just sat around feeling terrible, there was no way he was going to say no to a drink. A thick coat of dust covered the wood floors, the shelves were unorganized, signs crooked, and the paint faded.

The shop didn't open for another hour, so he began with the shelves. Some things needed to be restocked, some organized. The hooks were mixed together—jig heads with circle hooks—and there was no rhyme or reason to where they sat on the shelves. Like a puzzle, one by one he moved packets here and there, up and down, until all five shelves were weight, size, brand, and color coordinated. That alone took an hour, and by the time he was finished, it was six o'clock and time to open up shop.

Monday morning was always slow, and he didn't expect any customers. Usually, they were few and far between during the week. But just as the sun's first light rose above the horizon, a large diesel truck backed onto the boat ramp. Even in the low light, the neon green lettering was reflective enough for Clay to read the words scrawled on the side—'THE ALABAMA LARGEMOUTH'.

Sherman stumbled from his tall truck with two large coffees that billowed steam as he trudged forward. He moved just as much side to side as he did forward while he walked. The sight reminded Clay of a tall sportfishing boat in a rough ocean, the crow's nest seeming to touch the surface as it leaned back and forth. A mountain of a man walked behind him, coffee in hand as well. Sherman's cheeks were red, and he inhaled deep, long breaths as if'd he run a marathon. "Hey there, buddy!" he said as he barged through the front door. He held it open with his short, stubby foot as the man behind him shuffled in sideways.

Now that they were in the light, Clay recognized the giant boulder that stood in front of him, Bubba Lox. Although Clay graduated a year after Bubba began high school, he knew Bubba by reputation. He was the first eighth-grader to make the varsity football team. At the young age of thirteen, Bubba stood taller and wider than most of the seniors. By the time he was a freshman, he'd grown another two inches and was the largest man on the field, looking like he could run through a brick wall. Bubba skated through high school as a football star, guaranteed to go to a Division I football program on a full scholarship as a ruthless defensive lineman. He played professionally for two seasons in the United States, then another few in Canada. Clay couldn't recall where he went to college. He lived a few towns away, but he heard he got big into bass fishing after retirement.

Sherman slurped his coffee. "Clay, this little man right here is Bubba Lox. Bubba, Clay Booker."

"Bubba, nice to meet you."

"How's it goin'?" Bubba had a low voice and a bear paw grip that encapsulated Clay's hand.

"Bubba and I are gonna get some filmin' in this mornin' before it gets too hot. Hopefully find a fatty or two—oh, this is yours." Sherman handed the second cup to Clay. "You don't mind if we do a quick interview in here, do ya?"

Clay looked around the shop. He didn't have nearly enough time to finish cleaning the entire thing. "Why the hell do you want to do it in here?"

Sherman ignored his question. "Perfect! Here, I'm gonna need you to film it, I forgot my damn tripod." He handed over his phone to Clay, who stared at it with confusion, wondering how he'd become the cameraman.

He held it straight up and down, and Sherman directed him to turn it into the horizontal mode. "Just count down from three, Clay," Sherman said as he fixed his shirt and patted the large Bubba Lox, who towered over him. Just as soon as the camera began rolling, a wave of energy washed over Sherman. There were a lot of hand motions, 'booyahs!', smiles, and fast questions for the ex-football player. All the while, he mentioned Buoy's Marina, Bait and Tackle and how great it was. And just as quickly as the pre-fishing interview had begun, it was over. Sherman gave Clay a hug that caught him by surprise. "Thanks for the help, brother. Place looks good by the way." He patted Clay on the back. "Nice and organized. We'll talk later about how Sunday went. You're here, so at least she didn't kill ya! That's what I was worried about!"

"What?" Bubba asked.

"Worse, she made me go to church."

"Church? Good! You need the Lord in your life. Alright, we gotta go get on these things. I'm gonna be sweating like Clay in church by nine a.m." Sherman turned to Bubba and shook his head. "Let's get outta here. We'll catch up this afternoon, brother, thanks!"

Clay continued to work on the inside of the shop. He swept; he organized; he disinfected. A few more boats trickled into the marina for use of the ramp, but no one bought anything in the shop, and he noticed. The weight of the bank's letters continued to grow heavy on his shoulders. Now they weren't only going to take his business, but his family as well. The thought festered in the back of his mind.

By the time the sun rose, just about everyone who intended to fish that day was already out, and he took to the task. There was more work to accomplish than just knocking down a few nails. In the corner of the small barn, behind the covered boat, a tall stack of wooden boards sat collecting dust. As he walked past his father's boat, he whispered, "I'll get to you soon enough ol' girl. First things first."

He felt like he'd cut a thousand pieces by the time he finished the entire pile of lumber. Sweat soaked his shirt and burned his eyes as he gazed upon the crooked docks ahead of him. Having a drink of whiskey would have done him nice at that moment. Instead, he thought of Red and, with a stack of planks in his hand, headed toward the docks.

Clay's pink skin tingled with a slight sizzling sensation as he ripped the last board at the end of the dock. There wasn't a cloud in the sky, and the sun burned his nose and the back of his neck. With his hands on his hips, he smiled at his work. The planks were fresh and smooth, and if he didn't know any better, he would think it was a new dock.

His stomach grumbled, reminding him that he needed some food. Maybe it was also letting him know it was time for a drink. Out of nowhere, a piercing air horn rattled Clay's eardrums. He spun around to see Sherman and Bubba laughing on the boat like school children who had pranked their friend.

"What in the—the hell are y'all doin'?" Clay asked.

"Laughin' at you! What're you doin' out here? It's a thousand degrees out. I'd be shacked up inside readin' nudie mags or somethin'."

"I—"

Sherman noticed the refurbished dock. "Well, looky there! Brand-spankin'-new decking! That's what I'm talkin' about! Lookin' fancy!"

"How'd y'all do?"

Sherman backhand slapped Bubba on the chest. "Bubba got himself some buoys today!"

"Some buoys, huh?" Clay asked as he picked up his tools. "That sounds like a good day to me."

"We decided we're gonna adopt your use of the word 'buoy', Clay. It's got a real nice ring to it."

"Is that right?"

"Yeah, we caught too damn many fish today to stop sayin' it now. It's good luck."

"Shoot," Bubba said. "This place should be famous. There's some world class fishin' minutes away."

"Buoy Bait and Tackle… famous? Ha! I'll believe it when I see it."

CHAPTER 14

A HAUNTING PAST

Every day that week, Sherman came in to fish. And every day that week, after serving the few customers in the morning, Clay continued to fix up the marina with the little budget he had. He would pass the boat on the way for a tool and resisted the urge to tear off the tarp and begin fixing it up. That project was for he and Red to do together. He even cleaned his glorified closet and trimmed his beard to a manageable length. When Sunday morning came, he was church-ready. He paused as he stood in the silent shop, staring at his inventory. He snagged a pack of the purple flipping jigs he'd told Pastor Dave he liked the week before and stuffed them into his pocket.

With his collared shirt tucked into jeans, a belt, and freshly shined work boots, he couldn't stand to sit around for another second. So he left for Sunday service an hour early. The sweat on his palms made the steering wheel slippery, and he tapped his finger in a constant rhythm as he drove in silence.

With time to spare, his mind began to wonder. Maybe this was all for nothing; maybe it was too late. Maybe Red would never forgive him, and he would be alone for the rest of his life. Maybe they were better off without him. Abi would never forgive him. And why should she? He was a drunk. A deadbeat dad. Good for nothing but creating more problems in their life. The whiskey called his name with more and more ferocity.

The parking lot was empty except for Pastor Dave's truck, which was nicer and newer than Clay's. The front doors to the quaint church were closed but unlocked as he pushed them open. No one was inside except a statue of Jesus nailed to the cross, which hung at the front of the room. It seemed to stare into his soul as the swinging doors closed behind him. Clay tiptoed down the aisle of the empty room, trying to not make eye contact with the statue. "Pastor Dave? You there?"

No answer. Then, he heard a faint yell coming from the back of the church. Worried something might be wrong, Clay picked up the pace of his walk. "Pastor Dave?" he called again.

Another yell echoed through the church, growing louder as Clay made his way to the back. The pastor's voice was muffled by the walls, but his tone was frantic. Clay wasn't sure what he was about to walk into. As he opened the back door, there was Pastor Dave on the edge of a pond with a bass flopping on the shoreline. Dave yelled again with his hands up in the air like he had just won a championship. Clay sighed in relief.

"Clay!" Dave said. "What perfect timing! Come over, check this toad out! My biggest yet!" Dave's eyes were alive with excitement. He lifted the plump fish from the manicured grass and grinned from ear to ear.

Clay whistled through his front teeth. "That's a good'un, right there!" The pond behind the pastor was the size of a football field, and the surface was rippling uneasily from the battle between man and fish. The fish was a solid four pounds, a respectable fish for any body of water.

Pastor Dave kneeled on the shoreline, his knees wet and muddy. He caressed the fish with a gentle touch as he moved it back and forth in the water, helping it regain its strength before sending it back into its world with defined borders. "Ah, what a beautiful way to start the morning," he said to himself. "That was a true blessing."

"What'd you catch her on?"

"Worm and hook," Dave said as he picked up his rod from the grass and held a green plastic worm in his hand that was torn in half by the vicious bite of a largemouth bass. "I've found simplicity is key, not just in fishing, but in all aspects of life."

"Is that right? Huh. Just a worm and hook and that's all you plan on usin' from now on?"

"Well, it did just catch me my biggest bass yet. I'm sure that wasn't impressive for a guy like you, but for me, that was a trophy. Why would I change?" They began walking together back toward the church.

"That's a good point. So I guess you don't want these flippin' jigs I brought for ya?"

Dave's eyes widened. "Oh no, I'll take those. These are the ones you use?"

"I gotta be honest with ya, Dave. I haven't been out on the water much the last few years. I don't really use much of anything."

"What! I thought you owned that marina and bait shop—Buoy's!"

"I do, but I ain't done much fishin'. Haven't been doin' much of anything, really. Rottin' away mostly, what it feels like."

97

Dave stopped halfway to the backdoor of the church and grinned mischievously. "Well then, by all means, we must continue fishing."

"Church starts soon, don't it?"

Dave pushed the rod into Clay's chest. "I have an extra pole inside, get to fishin'. God wouldn't have had you get here an hour early if he didn't want you to fish." He broke into a jog as he headed back to the church, leaving Clay alone with nothing but the pond in front of him.

Clay twisted the plastic worm at eye level, making sure it was fish-ready. He cast out, and just as he struggled with his accuracy and the smoothness of his cast when he was with Sherman, he struggled here as well. The line inside of the baitcaster backlashed into a big knot inside of the reel, and Clay pulled out the knot as quickly as he could before Dave saw. He cast again and again. It was silent for the moment while he was alone, and the nervousness he felt before vanished. His shoulders lowered, and each cast became more fluid than the last.

Soon, Dave returned with another rod. "There's a steep ledge just off the shoreline they like to hang around," Dave said as he cast to the area. "That's where I just caught the—" He pulled his rod into his ribs, and it bent over as he reeled in a little one. "Oooh, ohhh, ohhh!" Dave said as he jumped back and forth while reeling in the fish. "It must be my morning!"

"Well, I guess I can't argue with results," Clay said he reeled in the worm. "I'm gettin' schooled." He cast in the same area and after two twitches, hooked up as well.

Dave released his catch as Clay reeled his in. "That feeling never gets old," he said with a hand on his hip.

Clay's fish was small enough to pull out of the water by the line. It wasn't even a pound. He tossed it back in the water and cast again. He smiled and laughed with Dave, who acted like it was the first fish ever caught every time either one of them hooked into one.

"Why'd you decide to start coming to church, Clay?"

"Well, I'd be lyin' if I said it was to get closer to God, Dave. And I ain't much of the lyin' type. My boy and his mom are part of the church here."

"Redmond and Abilene, yes. Wonderful kid, Red."

"I wouldn't really know. I haven't been in the picture, and well, I'm tryin' to change that. Comin' here is about the only place I can see Red right about now."

"You're a good person, Clay. You just went down the wrong path."

"I ain't a good person, Dave. If you knew half the things I've done, you wouldn't even let me inside."

"On the contrary, my friend. On the contrary."

Clay didn't say anything for a few minutes, only fished. "My dad was killed in a car accident ten years ago. It was rainin'. He wanted to drive, but I insisted on doing it. I hit a puddle goin' too fast. I—I just lost control. My dad died upside down in a ditch while I was saved." He shook his head. "Abi had Red nine months later."

"I remember." Dave cast. "It was an accident. It could've happened to anyone. No one's fault, only a tragic series of events."

"That's a nice way of lookin' at it, but I was drivin' and it was my fault."

"You have to forgive yourself, Clay. Your dad would want you to forgive yourself."

Clay didn't respond. He gazed over the lake, then laid into a bass that swallowed his bait.

Time went by, but neither noticed, nor cared. They were on a hot bite, and just as a gambling man never walks away from a heater, a fisherman never walks away from a hot bite.

"Pastor Dave!" someone yelled from behind them.

Dave froze as if he were a caught criminal, and turned around. "Yes?"

"It's time for service! Everyone's been lookin' for you!" It was an older man who was probably nagged by his wife into finding Dave.

"Is it that time already? We're coming!"

Clay had forgotten all about church in the midst of the bass bite. He wasn't sure if Dave had forgotten as well, or just didn't care. Dave winked at Clay. "One more cast."

Clay and Dave walked into church with fishing poles in hand as the entire congregation sat and glared. Dave leaned close to Clay and handed him his rod. "Put those in a corner somewhere…" He then raised his voice as he addressed the people of the congregation. "Sorry for being late folks! The newest member of our congregation, Clay Booker, was just showing me some fishing tips. Some of you may remember Clay from last week." The room was silent. "Clay, say hello!"

Embarrassed, he raised the two rods in the sky, as if to say hello. Abi and Red sat in the same spot they had the prior week. Abi had her head down with her hand on her forehead, but Red smiled with amusement at the sight of his dad standing on the stage with fishing rods in his hand. Hank crossed his arms across his chest and shook his head.

Clay stood there for a moment, and no one moved or said anything. "Find yourself a seat. We'll talk fishing later." Dave clapped once, signifying the beginning of the service.

As Clay walked down the quiet aisle, Red waved. "Hey, Dad!"

The people all turned in their seats toward Red.

"Hey, buddy. We'll talk later."

The whole reason he got to church early was to find a seat closer to Red. Since he'd gotten distracted fishing, that plan went out the window. He placed the rods in the corner of the room and ended up sitting in the same seat in the back. This time, he was next to an old man with mountainous wrinkles and dark eyes that had seen many things. He wore a pink button-down shirt that his wife made him wear by the looks of it.

"Did y'all catch anything?" the old man asked Clay. But before Clay could answer, the man's wife slapped him on the shoulder.

Dave began the service, and Clay tried to pay attention the best he could. Red continued checking on his father, probably to make sure he was still there. Each time, Abi, without looking behind her, turned Red forward again.

Once the service was over, unlike the prior week, Abi took her time getting up and getting her things together. Bill and Sue passed Clay with a smile, something he wasn't used to. Clay stood on the edge of the aisle and let the congregation pass him on their way out as he waited. Red waved at him again. Abi kept a hand on her son's shoulder as she spoke with another couple. After a few minutes of talking, Abi's conversation finished, and only a few people lingered in the room.

Red ran out of his mother's grasp and embraced Clay with the tightest squeeze he could muster. "I knew you'd come back," he said, face pressed against his dad's stomach. "Hank and Mom didn't think so, but I did."

As his son hugged him, a lump formed in Clay's throat, and his eyes filled with tears. "Of course, I was gonna come back. I ain't goin' anywhere." He closed his eyes and hugged his son even tighter.

"Okay... okay." Abi patted Red's back.

Hank stood behind her, arms crossed. "That's enough."

Clay opened his eyes, and tears fell down his cheek. But as fast as they fell, he rubbed them away. "Hey."

"Hello," she said with her arms crossed and shoulders hunched as she stared at her son, who was fixated on his father. "About last week, I'm sorry I—"

Hank rolled his eyes. "Jeez, Abi, I told you not to apologize."

"Hank Monroe, right? Clay Booker. We met a long time ago."

"I know who you are. I know all about you and what you've done. I'm surprised you even remember us meeting." Abi seemed confused. "Buoy's Marina, Bait and Tackle is mortgaged through Acreage, baby," he said to Abi. "But not for much longer."

Clay clenched his fist and took a deep breath. He wanted nothing more than to knock Hank out right then and there. "Don't be sorry, Abi. I showed up unannounced I— it was my fault. The whole thing, everything. I know I don't deserve it, but if you could just give me a chance, I'll show Red—show both of you—that I want to be here. I'm trying to change for the better."

"I forgive you, Dad."

Abi pressed her lips together. "You have a lot to prove to Red. I want you to be around for him. I really do."

"Did you guys catch anything, Dad?"

Dave had just finished talking to a member of the congregation who was concerned by the fact that they'd started service late two weeks in a row, and now jumped into the conversation. "Oh, did we catch 'em Redmond! I bet they're still bitin', too!"

"Really? Can I go try to catch one?"

"That's up to your mom," Clay said.

Red, Clay, and Dave all looked at Abi like begging puppies. With her lips still pressed together, she paused like she was thinking.

"Please, mom? Please, please." Red tugged at her sundress.

Hank spoke up. "I don't think so—"

Abi interrupted Hank. "Only for a few minutes. We're supposed to have lunch with your—"

Red heard the okay from his mom, and that was all he needed. He ran, grabbed one of the rods, and was already heading to the back door. He stopped half way down the aisle and looked back at his parents, who were both staring at him with smiles. "What're you doin', Dad? Let's go!"

Dave, who was almost as excited as Red, picked up the other rod. "There's some big'uns waiting for us out there, Redmond!" He rushed past Clay and Abi just as fast as Red did, and with an equal amount of gusto.

"Thank you," Clay said to Abi.

"I'm doing this for Red, not for you. I just hope this is real and you're not going to disappear, for Red's sake."

"Abi I—"

"Hank and I will be waiting here. Please be careful."

"We're only fishing, Abi."

"Not careful about fishing, be careful of Red. Don't hurt him again."

Clay swung open the back door of the church. Red and Dave already had their lines in the water. "Dad, I just got a bite!" Red said as he held the rod. "C'mon!"

Clay stood next to his son and gave him pointers as he fished. They laughed, and a few minutes in, Red hooked a little bass, but reacted like he caught a marlin. He jumped in excitement as he pulled the fish onto shore, and Clay and Dave were just as excited for him.

Clay gave his son a high five. "Atta boy!"

"I did it! I did it! I caught my own bass!"

"Good job, buddy!" Dave said.

Clay kneeled down, picked up the bass with his thumb by its mouth, and pulled out the hook. "You wanna hold it?"

"Yes!"

Red held it just as his father did, admiring the green water creature and studying every detail of it. Then, he turned and showed his mom and Hank, who were sitting on a bench next to the church, watching. Abi gave him two thumbs up.

"Alright, now put it back down in the water so it can grow big and you can catch it again one day." With the gentlest touch, Red dropped down to both knees and let the bass swim into the depths of the pond.

"That was awesome."

"Yeah it was!" Clay said. "Let's catch another."

"Not if I do first," Dave said, as he cast over the top of Red, who was still sitting, staring at the water in amazement.

Red and Clay walked the edge of the lake. Clay showed Red where to cast and how to twitch the rod just the way bass liked it. They laughed and joked. Clay was as happy as he had ever been. As they were almost finished with a full lap around the lake, Abi waved her hands signaling it was time to go.

Dave continued to fish as they walked up to Abi. "It's about time to go, honey."

"Can I just stay for another five minutes?"

"You heard your mom. Let's go," Hank said impatiently.

"No, I'm sorry sweetie, your grandparents are waiting for us. Did you have fun?"

"Yeah! We caught a bunch of big bass! It was awesome. Dad showed me how to hold a bass by its mouth—" Red talked without catching his breath. "Look at this." He held up his thumb, which was pink, and the top layer of skin was missing. It looked as if he'd rubbed sandpaper against it.

"Oh, are you okay?"

"Yeah, that's just from holding all the bass. Dad says that's how you know you've had a good day of fishin'." Clay smiled and shrugged.

"I think we have Band-Aids in the car. Go on and find one, I'll be there in a minute. I have to talk to your dad."

"Okay." Red turned and hugged his dad. "I love you, Dad. Thanks for taking me fishing."

"I love you too, buddy. Listen to your mom, now. I'll see you soon."

"Okay. You're not going to leave again, are you?"

105

Clay squatted down into a baseball catcher's position. "No, I'm not going anywhere, I promise."

Abi crossed her arms and turned to Hank. "You too, honey."

"You sure?"

"Yeah, I'm fine." He whispered something in her ear, then kissed her a little longer than he should have. He stared at Clay, didn't say anything, then made his way back into the church.

"So…" Abi said.

"Yeah?"

"What're your intentions here?"

"My intentions?"

"Yeah, do you plan on sticking around? Or is this just a one time thing."

"No… no of course not, Abi. I ain't leavin'. I just want to be in Red's life. That's all."

Abi looked down and kicked around the marshy dirt on the pond's bank. "I want you to be in Red's life, too. But I don't want you to get his hopes up. Things are goin' pretty well right now, Clay. And honestly, I don't want you to mess that up for us."

"Look, I quit drinkin'. I'm tryin' my best to fix up the marina with the little money I got. I'm tryin' to better my-self. I know you don't trust me. But if you can just give me a chance, all I ask is for a few hours every week to begin with. We can do it after church if you want. Or whenever, it don't matter to me."

"Okay… okay, fine. If you continue coming, you can see Red afterward, as long as I'm close by and you're sober. After all the shit you've pulled, you're lucky I'm even con-sidering that."

CHAPTER 15

EVEN IF THE BASS ARE BITIN'

Clay fell into a routine that he grew to love. He worked at the marina, helping the few customers that came in, and tried his best to make the place look presentable, as it had when his father ran it. The dirt stained windows were cleaned, wood on the docks replaced, and the grass mowed. He even repainted the outside of the shop in a crisp white. Every Sunday, Clay went to church, and he, Red, and Dave would fish afterward. Abi slowly found an inkling of trust in him.

Early one Sunday morning, Clay woke up to Abi calling him on his cellphone. "Hello?" Clay asked as he answered the phone.

"Hey, sorry for calling so early, but I have an issue."

Clay sprang up. "Is everything okay?"

"Everything is fine. I just got called into work—one of the waitresses quit. I have to go cover. Hank is out of town on business, and my parents took a weekend trip to the coast. Is there any way you could come over early and take Red to church with you?"

"Yeah, no problem. Of course. I'm throwin' on some clothes, then I'll be over."

"And Clay?"

"Yeah?"

"I'm trying my best to trust you, but I'm worried. You haven't been drinking have you?"

"I haven't had a drink in weeks. I promise. Me and Red are gonna have a great day. I'm really looking forward to it."

"Okay… I'll see you soon then."

It wasn't long after Clay knocked on the front door of Abi's house that the first rays of light poked just above the horizon. He held a big paper bag from a fast-food restaurant in one hand. "Hey," she said as she let him in. "He's still asleep."

"Oh, gotcha. You hungry? I got breakfast." Clay looked around. He hadn't been inside her parents' house in years.

"No, I'm okay. I gotta go. I'd wake up Red here in a few minutes. Thank you so much for coming over."

"Anytime you need me, I'm here."

"Be careful, please."

"We will."

Abi smiled and walked out the front door. With his hands in his pockets, he walked around the living room as if he were in a museum and didn't want to touch anything. Around the outdated box television were family pictures of Red, Abi, Sue, Bill, and even Hank. He didn't expect to see himself in any of those pictures, but it was as if he didn't exist in their lives, and it hurt.

Red's door was cracked open, and Clay felt weird being alone in the house any longer, so he tiptoed into his room. Red was curled up in a ball of covers and didn't budge when Clay walked in. Toys laid across his floor, apparently from a big Saturday the night before. He was careful to walk around the toys and not make any noise. On the desk sat school textbooks and a pack of plastic worms and hooks. As his eyes scanned the area, his heart dropped. There was proof that he existed in this house after all. On the corner of the desk was a small, framed picture of he and Red holding a bass together. He remembered that day, and the memory brought him to tears as he held up the picture.

"Dad?"

Clay turned with the picture in his hand and wiped his face. "Hey, buddy."

"What're you doing here?"

"Your mom had to go to work. Just me and you goin' to church today."

Red rubbed his eyes and smiled. "Can we just go fishin'?"

"I wish. I promised your mom we'd go to church. We can fish in the pond with Pastor Dave afterward. You hungry?"

"Whatcha got?"

"Egg and cheese sandwiches, donuts, hash browns, all the good stuff."

Red's eyes widened, and he rolled out of bed. Clay put the picture down and followed behind his hungry son. They laughed as they ate, and Clay tried soaking up every last second alone with his son. He looked down and dropped his sandwich onto his plate. "Hey, buddy, I got somethin' to say."

"Yeah?" Red asked, with a mouthful of donut.

"I never apologized for leaving you and your mom. And I just want you to know that I'm sorry for the things I've done in the past. I can't change any of that, but I'm going to try and be the best dad I can be now."

Red nodded. "Mom told me not to be mad at you. That you had some stuff to figure out, but you still loved me."

Clay's face turned red. He looked down and tried to not show Red the grin he had on his face. He took another bite of his sandwich and ruffled his hand over his son's hair. He was just glad Abi hadn't told Red to hate him forever. "Well, shoot. I always have and always will love ya. I'm trying my best to figure it out, buddy. I wasn't always there for ya, but I will be from now on. Even if the bass are bitin'." He winked at his son, and they bumped knuckles.

Bill walked into the house with two bags of luggage on his arms. He stopped at the front door and put down the bags. "Well, hello there."

"Hey Pop-Pop," Red said with a mouthful of donut.

"Where's your mother at?"

"She got called into work," Clay said.

"Oh, what a pleasant surprise," Sue said as she entered the house.

"Abi had to work," Bill said to his wife.

"It's a good thing we came home early then! We'll take you to church, darlin'," Sue said as she kissed Red on the forehead.

"No, that's okay. Abi called me over to take him to-day."

"Oh, did she?" Sue asked. "Well, we're here now. So that won't be necessary. You can meet us over there, though."

Red looked up at his Dad. "I want to go with Dad."

"You go get ready, sugar pie. I want to speak with your father."

"Okay." Red took one last bite of a donut and ran to his room. Bill retreated to his room with the luggage as well.

"Look, Clay. It's nice and all that you've been comin' to church. Obviously, Abi had no other choice but to call you over here. You're more than welcome to join us. But I don't think you're ready to have alone time with Red just yet. What's it been, a few weeks since you've come back into our lives?"

"Somethin' like that."

"Not long enough to earn alone time, in my opinion."

Clay took a seat at the kitchen table. "I appreciate everything you've done for Red. You've been there for him when I wasn't. But I'm here now, and I ain't goin' nowhere. That's my son in there. I'm tryin' my best to get my shit together for him and Abi. Not for you, not for Bill, or anyone else. I'm around for good, whether you like it or not. And I feel like I've earned enough privilege to take my own damn son to church."

Sue sat down next to Clay with a worried look on her face and cupped her hand in his. "All those nights you weren't here,—and even the nights you were here before you left them—Bill and I were the ones who Abi cried to. We were the ones who supported her and Red. And you were nowhere to be found. Do you know what I see happening now?"

"No, I don't."

"I'm seeing the same thing that I saw before. Giving Red and Abi an inkling of hope that you'll be a good father, but I think you're weak. You're weak, and with one misstep, you'll be back drinking again and nowhere to be found. You were twenty minutes away for the last three years, and there were times when Abi wanted to go see you and beg for you to come back into their lives. I'm the one who told her that she couldn't do that. That the only way you would ever work out for them was if you wanted to be here with them."

"And I'm here. Now. I wanted to be with them every day. But... I couldn't. I felt like they were better off without me. But I was wrong. You have to trust me. I want to be with them. I've always wanted to be with them, I just needed some time, I guess."

Sue grabbed his hand in hers. "They weren't better off without you, Clay. You have a lot of problems, but this is the happiest I've seen Red in a long time, Abi as well. It's hard, really hard, but I'm going to trust you because Abi obviously has found a little trust in you and I have to support her decisions as a mother."

Red ran out of his room ready for church. "I'm ready!"

"So is your father. We'll see you two over there."

CHAPTER 16

BUMP IN THE ROAD

Clay and Red went to church and fished with Dave in the pond afterward. Abi walked out of the backdoor of the church just as they finished fishing. They were on the other side of the pond and walked back with their fishing rods in hand. The next day was Red's first day of school. "You have fun today?"

"Yeah, it was fun."

"Something wrong, buddy?"

"Dad, can I live with you?"

Clay was quiet. The back of the tackle shop was no place for a human to live, let alone a kid. "You don't like living with your mom?"

"I do, but I don't wanna go to school."

"Why not?"

"All the other kids don't like me. I just wanna live with you and fish every day."

"Fishin' ain't goin' nowhere, son. School's important, and bein' with your mom is important, too. She needs you. Why don't the other kids like you?"

"They make fun of me all the time and call me a nerd 'cause I get good grades. I don't wanna be a nerd anymore. I don't wanna go back. Can I please just stay with you?"

"As much as I would love that, buddy, you can't. You have to go to school, and you have to live with your mama." Red sighed, just as his father did. "And let me tell you something, son. Some people don't like hard work. They may make fun of ya, call you a nerd. But the truth is, people envy hard work. They're intimidated by it because they know deep down they don't have the guts to do it themselves. I should know, I've been one of those people my entire life. But that ain't you, Red. And I couldn't be more proud of ya, son. Keep workin' hard, it'll all pay off one day, I promise. And on the weekends, you can catch monster bass with your ol' dad."

"Okay, I guess."

"And if one of those kids makes fun of you, make fun of them back."

"I don't know what to say."

"Call 'em idiots. Tell 'em you'll beat their ass if they keep talkin'."

Red opened his eyes wide. "Mom says I should never fight."

"Never start a fight, son. But if they keep makin' fun of you, hit them right there." Clay pointed between Red's eyes. "They'll quit talkin' then."

"Can you not tell mom? She just makes it worse and makes me look like a snitch."

"A snitch?" Clay paused. "I won't tell her. Just remember what I said, right between the eyes."

"Hey there, honey. Did you have a good morning?"

"Me and dad have been catchin' 'em all mornin'!"

"Yeah? And how was church?"

"Oh, that was fun, too." Clay walked up behind him and smiled.

"That sounds awesome! Are you hungry?"

"I'm so hungry."

"Well, then, say bye to your dad, and we'll go pick something up."

Clay scratched the back of his head with his chin down. "I'll see ya next week, buddy."

It was obvious Clay wanted to join them, but he didn't dare ask. "Would you like to join?" Abi asked.

"Hank ain't gonna mind?"

"Yeah, Dad, come!"

"I think it'll be fine if you tag along."

"Can we get Ranch's?" Red asked. Ranch's Barbeque was a quaint lunch and dinner spot that had a tangy sauce and the best barbeque in Okeechobee County—the locals said it was the best barbeque in the *country*. It also was the restaurant that Abi and Clay used to frequent before they had Red.

"Ranch's sounds good to me," Abi said.

Red turned to his dad for approval. "Yeah, Ranch's it is. Haven't had it in years."

"Really?" Abi asked. "That was your favorite place."

"Well, it was my favorite place to go with you."

Red and Abi sat across from Clay. As they sat down, Clay and Red did the same thing, unbeknownst to either of them. They both plopped into the booth, sighed, ran their hands through their hair and leaned their elbows on the table. They ate wings and ribs, and they laughed as Red's face was covered in barbeque sauce. Clay could only smile. He hadn't done something with the two of them in a long time, and he was overjoyed. "So, I've done a lot of fixin' up at the marina," he said as he wiped his face with a wet napkin.

"Oh, yeah?" Abi asked. "That's great."

"Yeah, I got it lookin' at least presentable now. But there is one last thing that needs fixin' up."

"What is that?"

"My pop's old bass boat. I thought maybe Red and I could fix it up together."

Red looked to his mom for approval, but she shook her head. "I don't think so, darling," she said to Red. He and Clay's faces dropped in disappointment. "I don't have time for that right now. I barely have time to go to church as it is."

"But, mom."

"I'll pick him up, drop him off. You don't have to do anything at all. C'mon, Abi," Clay said.

"I'm sorry, it's just not gonna happen right now. Hank and I both agreed that church is enough. Maybe some time in the future."

After lunch, Clay drove home feeling more defeated than ever. He thought he had made progress with Abi and Red over the past weeks. She trusted him to come over that morning; Sue said she trusted him. It appeared to be enough progress for her to trust him to be alone with Red during the day on the weekends, but she didn't trust him any more than she did the first Sunday when she tried running him over. He felt helpless, hopeless, and ready for a drink. He might as well drink if she was never going to let his son be with him.

He mashed the gas pedal down the long two lane road that cut through barbed wire cattle farm back toward Lake Okeechobee. He came upon a semitruck driving too slowly for him and attempted to pass, but a car approached from the opposite lane. There wasn't enough time for him to pass the semi. His eyebrows narrowed together, and, with white knuckles, he accelerated around the semi, head-to-head with the other car. The car's driver held down his horn as they approached, now only feet away from one another. The semitruck driver slammed on his brakes, and the opposing car ran off the road and wrecked into the fence. With locked brakes, the semi skidded to a halt, its trailer fishtailing sideways into the middle of the road. Clay turned back into his lane, almost lost control, then continued to speed on like nothing happened.

Instead of stopping at the marina, he drove past it and pulled into the liquor store he used to frequent. "Dammit," he said as he ran his hands over his face. He got out of his truck and soon was leaving the liquor store grasping a brown bag that covered a bottle of whiskey. He gripped the bottle with the same ferocity as he did the steering wheel while he drove back to the marina.

As he pulled into the parking lot, he twisted open the cap to his bottle. Suddenly, he stopped, spotting the dad and son he had helped a few weeks ago. They were washing down their boat, and the father waved at Clay as he left his truck.

"Hey man, I just left the money for usin' the ramp under the doormat."

"No problem." He took the five dollar bill from under the mat and gave it back to the man. "Don't worry about it. I wasn't here anyway."

"Well, thank you. I can't tell ya how much I appreciated the help a little while ago. Jake here got to catch his biggest bass yet. Tell him Jake!"

"It was huge! Like a dinosaur! It's mouth was as big as my head!" The kid held out his hands as wide as he could. "It was this big."

The dad chuckled and ruffled his son's hair. "We really appreciate it."

"Glad to hear it." Clay gave half a smile. "Y'all have a good rest of your day." He opened the shop door and disappeared inside. As he propped up his feet behind the register and opened the bottle, he watched the dad and son finish cleaning their boat. He imagined he and Red doing the same with their boat after a day of fishing. That thought made him happier than whiskey ever had, and he dumped the bottle down the sink.

CHAPTER 17

WHERE RED
GETS IT FROM

The next day started as any other—hot, and not much of anything happening around the marina. Clay set up paper plate targets across the shop and practiced pitching baits toward them. He swayed the plastic crawdad back and forth as if it were on a pendulum. He was out of practice and grew frustrated every time he missed the target. There was a time where he could hit a spot the size of a quarter from a hundred feet away.

His phone vibrated on the counter and threw off his concentration as he flipped the bait toward a target and missed completely. "Dammit, who in the hell?" He checked his phone; it was a local number he didn't recognize.

"Hello?"

A woman with a strong and stern voice answered. "Hello, this is Shandra Brown, the Principal of Okeechobee Elementary School. Is this Mister Clay Booker?"

Clay stiffened. "Yeah, what's wrong?"

"You are listed as an emergency contact for Redmond."

"I am?"

"Well, you're the very last contact. We tried reaching everyone on his list with no success."

"Is Red okay?"

"Your son has engaged in an altercation with another student. He needs to be picked up immediately. He has been suspended for a week."

"I'll be right there."

Clay rushed to the school. He couldn't believe his name was on the contact list, but he was happy it was. As he walked into the principal's office, there sat Red. He leaned far into his seat with his arms crossed, a black eye, and an upset look on his face, as if he were about to cry. "Hey, buddy." Clay smiled at his son. "You alright?" Red shook his head 'yes' but didn't say a word. "What does the other guy look like?" Red smiled, but quickly changed his expression as the principal glared at him.

"Excuse me, I am Principal Brown. Your son is in very big trouble, Mr. Booker. This is no smiling matter. We are only a week into the school year and your son—"

"Did you start the fight, son?"

"It does not matter, we do not condone—"

"Red is more than capable of explainin' the situation to me, ma'am. Thank you. Did you start the fight?"

"No." Red lowered farther into his seat. "He's been messin' with me since last year."

"Explain 'messin' with you'," Clay said.

"Callin' me names, pushin' me around. And I decided I ain't gonna take his shit anymore."

"Redmond Booker!" the principal exclaimed. "I will not stand for such language in this institution!"

Clay smiled, proud as could be. "Atta boy." He winked at his son and hit knuckles.

Appalled that Clay had not reprimanded his son as she expected, she slammed her fist on the desk. "This is a serious matter, Mr. Booker! He is suspended for a week, and I have half a mind to suspend him for another few days for cursing on school property!"

Clay let out a sarcastic laugh. "Shandra, I ain't goin' to reprimand my son for stickin' up for himself. He's been havin' issues with bullies at this school since he started, and he finally stuck up for himself. You do what you have to do, miss. But my son and I are leavin'. C'mon, Red, let's go fishin'."

As they got into Clay's truck, Abi called. "Hey, I just got off the phone with the school. They told me what happened. Where are you?" She sounded frantic, as any mother would be when her child was in trouble.

"We're just gettin' in my truck. I was gonna call Sherman, see if we can't go fishin' this afternoon."

"Fishing? Clay, are you kidding? He was just suspended. He's not going fishing. I'm going to try and get off early. I can't get a hold of Hank, but take Red over there. He should be home. Red knows how to get there."

"Hank? He can just stay with me, I'll take him home later."

"No, I want him with Hank. You can see him Sunday at church."

Clay hung up the phone and drove out of the parking lot. "Well, your momma don't want you goin' fishin'. Said you have to go to Hank's."

"But I wanna go fishin'."

"Yeah, me too. But what momma says, goes."

"Am I in trouble?"

"Not with me, you ain't. You have to stand up for yourself, or people like that will walk all over you. You get him good?"

"Yeah, I gave him a bloody nose, and he started to cry and ran away."

"That's my boy."

As they pulled up to Hank's house, Red sighed. "Can I just stay with you."

"I wish you could, buddy. C'mon, I'll walk you up."

There were two cars in the driveway. One was Hank's, and the other Red didn't recognize. Loud music blared from the house as they knocked on the door. No one answered, so Clay knocked harder and longer with his fist. Hank finally opened the door, with nothing but underwear and a cowboy hat on. His eyes widened as he made eye contact with Clay and Red. "Redmond? What're you doing here?"

"What the hell is going on here?" Clay asked.

A woman in her bra and underwear came up behind Hank and put her arms around his waist before resting her head on his shoulder. "Who are they?" she asked. "Come back to bed, baby."

Clay's fists clenched, and he began to shake. His eyes did not blink as they dialed in on Hank like a predator sighting prey. Without thinking, Clay smashed his forehead into Hank's nose. The woman screamed and ran into the back of the house. Hank fell to the ground, gripping his now-bloody nose. He groaned in pain. Clay took one step inside his house, fell to a knee, and loaded his arm back, ready to hit him with another blow.

"Clay!" He stopped and looked behind him. Abi stood in her waitress uniform behind Red.

"You're lucky," Clay said he stood up.

"What in the hell is going on?" Abi asked. Hank wallowed on the floor as he held his nose and groaned.

"Go on and tell her!" Clay said as he nudged Hank with his boot.

The woman in underwear ran out of the bedroom with a bat in her hand. Abi saw what was going on. "You piece of shit," she said as she stormed into the house and kicked Hank in the ribs. Then, she looked up at the woman, who was ready to hit Abi. "Honey, by the looks of it, you're going to need a lot more than that to stop me. Now put that thing down before you get yourself hurt over this moron. Let's go, Red."

"Abi, wait," Hank said as he propped himself up.

"Screw you, Hank. It's over."

Clay smiled at Hank and shrugged, then followed Abi and Red back to her car. With a remorseless look on her face, she got into her car, put sunglasses on, and rolled down her window as Red got into the back.

"Hey, I'm sorry for that, I just saw what was goin' on and—"

"Don't be sorry. He got what he deserved. Thank you for standing up for me. And I wonder where Red gets it from." She paused for a moment. "I'll drop Red off at the shop tomorrow. If he's not going to go to school for a week, he might as well learn how to redo a boat. As long as you can take him home at night, I'm okay with it—if that's okay with you." Red's face brightened up and he nodded in excitement to his dad.

"I'd love that."

CHAPTER 18

LET'S DO THIS THING

The next day started Labor Day weekend, and Abi dropped off Red. Clay had done a nice job of fixing the place up, and she noticed. It was old, but clean. Red ran out of his mom's car to his dad, who walked out of the shop. His backpack bounced back and forth as he ran across the parking lot. He gave his dad a big hug, as he always did.

"What's all this?"

"Clothes and stuff. Mom said I could stay the night!"

"If it's alright with you," Abi said.

"I'll have to make some room in the back, but heck yeah, buddy. You can stay the whole week if you want." Red looked at his mom for approval.

"Oh no, not the whole week, I can't go that long without you. But tonight will be okay."

"We're gonna have some fun, ain't we?" Clay said, and they smacked knuckles. "Go put your stuff up in the back, I have big day planned for us." Red ran into the shop with his backpack.

"How're you doing?" Clay asked.

Abi's cheeks turned pink. "I'm okay, I'm just more embarrassed than anything. I didn't mean to get you involved in all of that."

124

"I'm glad I did."

"It was pretty funny seeing him roll around on the ground moaning and groaning like that." They laughed and looked down like a teenage couple who didn't know what to say next. "Thank you for sticking up for me."

"I'd do it a thousand times over again," Clay said. She looked up at him with big innocent brown eyes. She was the most beautiful thing Clay had ever seen.

"Well, come on in, not much is goin' on right now anyway. Most everybody goin' fishin's already out." Abi followed him into the shop. "Not much has changed. I've been doin' some organizin', consolidatin'... stuff like that. Still needs a lot of work, but it's comin' along, I guess." They walked into the back room where Red held a fishing rod in his hand like a baseball player would to admire a brand new baseball bat. "I don't know if you remember, but it's a little cramped in here. You can take the bed tonight, Red. I got an air mattress somewhere we can blow up."

Abi crossed her arms, worried about Clay and his living situation. But she decided not to say anything because she could tell he was trying to get his life together. "Alright, I'll let you two be. I have some errands to run." She hugged Red and kissed him on the forehead. "If you need anything, call me, okay?"

"Okay."

"Be safe, please. Both of you. Keep your dad out of trouble."

"I will."

"Alright, I love you." She hugged her son and continued to hold him.

"I love you too... You can let go now, mom."

125

"I'm sorry." She stood. "Don't do anything too dumb with him, please."

"We'll be fine. Thank you for lettin' him come over."

"No problem." Abi left before Clay or Red could see the sporadic tears run down her cheek.

"You wanna see the boat?" Clay asked.

"Yeah!"

"C'mon, it's around back."

The gravel crunched under their shoes as they walked toward the barn. The doors creaked as Clay slid them open. As he stepped inside, he heard the scurrying of rats as they made a quick dash to their crevices and out of sight. Two large dim lights hung from the ceiling and buzzed as he turned them on.

He ripped off the tarp. He couldn't help but think of his dad. He smiled because he knew his father looked down and would be happy to see his son and grandson using it again.

Clay leaned on the side and looked into the boat, studying each and every little detail. Red studied his dad's movements and copied him, only he was on the tip of his toes in order to see over the side. The carpet was the first thing that needed to go. It was dry-rotted, and it crumbled as he ran his hand over it. "Your grandpa loved this thing. It's a shame he only got to use it once. But we're going to get plenty of use out of it. It's gonna be a lot of hard work at first, though. Are you ready for that?"

"Yes sir!" Red said. "As long as we don't sink again."

Clay paused. Chills ran down his spine from his past actions. "That ain't gonna happen," he said, and it was silent for a moment. "I think what we need to do first is get this nasty carpet up. What do you think?" Red nodded in agreement. Clay pulled out a pocket knife, "We'll start from the front deck and pull everything back."

Red climbed into the boat like a monkey up a tree, but Clay hesitated. Maybe he should just call Abi back and have her pick up Red.

"Are you getting up, Dad?"

"You still trust me after everything I put you and your mom through? You still even love me?"

Red sat down on the side of the boat and hugged his dad. "I'm always gonna love you, Dad. Just like you're always gonna to love me. You're not the same person that you were then. I can feel it."

Clay hoped he was right, but he wasn't as sure as his son was. "I love you too, buddy. Let's do this thing."

Clay cut around the sides, and they pulled off all the black carpet from the bow to the stern. The fiberglass deck had some stress cracks in it, but the integrity was solid. The hole in the front deck, chewed through by rats, was larger than it appeared when the carpet was on. They opened all the hatches and wiped everything down until it was dust free. It was hard work, but they laughed as they went along and enjoyed each other's company.

The barn blocked the little wind that rolled outside. Clay wiped sweat from his forehead as he sat on the bucket seat behind the steering wheel. Red had an old rag in his hand as he sat on the front deck. They both felt exhausted. "I think that's good for now. We'll get all that fiberglass work done next. Let's get some food, I'm starvin'." With dirt stains from his face to his feet, Red agreed.

That night, a large, lifted pink Ford diesel truck pulled into the parking lot as Clay and Red ate dinner at the base of the first dock. The bright pink truck with chrome rims and accents was pulling a shiny, black trailer. In large pink lettering across the back window was stenciled

"TheAlabamaLargemouth.com". Sherman drove and honked the horn and held it for too long as they parked in front of the bait shop. A robust woman stepped down a bit awkwardly from the truck, and they wondered how she did that every day. She had platinum blonde hair and was wearing a white cowboy hat, black, mirrored, aviator-style sunglasses, a tight pink shirt, blue jeans, and white boots.

"Well, hello!" she blurted out with her arms spread wide, not hesitating one bit to go in for a hug, even though Red had never met her before. He almost looked scared as she embraced him like a bear. "You must be Red!" She held his shoulders but took a step back to see the entirety of him. "You look like your pop! Holy cow!"

Sherman leaned over to the passenger side window. "Let the kid go, Caroline. You're scarin' him!"

"Oh shut up!" she said as she patted Red. And then her attention changed, and she forgot about Red altogether. "Clay, I'm lovin' the beard darlin'!"

"Thanks, Caroline," Clay said, happy to take the compliment. "What're you doin' here?"

"I was thinkin'!" Sherman said from the truck window. "You need a trailer for your boat! That thing you got it on now's gonna rust away any second! But forget that, come jump in—check this rig out!"

"What? A new trailer?"

"Jump in, I'll tell ya!"

Clay got in the passenger seat and Red in the back. Sherman turned behind him to face Red. "Hey, bud, I'm Sherman, an old friend of your dad's. Look at ya, all grown up. You're gonna be able to beat up your dad in no time. You can probably already out-fish him."

The interior was all white, with pink stitching and accents. There were two large, pink fuzzy balls that dangled from the rearview mirror. "This thing is ridiculous," Clay said as he looked around, stunned by his surroundings.

"I like it!" Red said from the back seat.

"It's Caroline's. I hated it just as much as you at first, but I gotta admit, this thing gets attention. I have a lot of fans that said they saw my website on this truck and ended up subscribin' to my stuff. Shoot, I'll do just about anything to get a few subscribers. Where you wanna put this thing?" he asked.

"Back it in next to the barn, I guess."

Sherman whipped the pink truck around and backed the trailer feet away from the outside of the barn. The wheel of the trailer scraped against a beam, and the entire barn vibrated. "Whoops," Sherman said as he pulled forward, hit the pole again, then readjusted. He parked the trailer behind the barn so that no one would know it was there. They got out of the truck and walked into the barn.

Caroline waddled on her high heels as she followed behind the boys. "How long is it gonna take?" Red asked as they stared at the boat.

"Eh, we'll work on it when we can. No need to rush, maybe have it done by Christmas."

"Screw that. Let's get this thing finished in time for the Lake O Extravaganza."

"Yeah darlin', that's what I'm talkin' about!" Caroline said.

Clay laughed to himself. "Yeah, sure." Sherman didn't respond, only stood there, unphased. Red had a big smile on his face as he stood behind his dad. "You're serious?"

"Dead serious."

"Shoot, Sherman. Even if we did have this thing up and runnin', which is a big 'if', I can't compete in a tournament. I've fished the lake once in how many years?"

"Who cares if you finish dead last. You know how proud your dad would be to see you fishin' a tournament out of his boat?" Clay stared at the carpet without a response. "Hey, buddy, I didn't mean that in a bad way."

"Dad, we can do it!" Red said. "That would be so cool!"

"Tell 'em, Red! It would be cool. No reason why we shouldn't."

"Can we talk about this over a plate of ribs? I am witherin' away over here," Caroline said.

"I think you'll survive a few missed meals," Sherman said.

"Oh, you're one to talk, man boobs."

"We can have it done and out catchin' fatties in a few weeks, no problem. Oh excuse me, buoys, I mean," Sherman said. "But momma's hungry, so I gotta go."

CHAPTER 19

THE BEYONCÉ
OF BASS FISHING

Over the next three weeks, they worked tirelessly every chance they had. There was a bit of a learning curve. Clay hadn't worked with fiberglass before, and rewiring all the electronics took a week after he accidentally shocked himself. Sherman and Red were there the day he shocked himself, and they fell to the floor laughing. The bilge pumps and batteries were replaced. The wiring for the entire boat was redone. They patched the hole in the deck with fiberglass and filled in the crack on the side, then painted black over it. They couldn't get a perfect black-and-red sparkle match, but from a distance, you couldn't tell anything had happened. As for the old, rusted trolling motor, there was no saving it. Rats had eaten through the wiring, and essential parts were rusted and unusable. Clay bought a brand new, remote controlled Minn Kota trolling motor with the money that he was supposed to send to the bank. The engine surprisingly started without too much of a hassle, which was a miracle in itself. Clay cleaned and lubricated every inch of the motor, replaced spark plugs, drained the old oil and fuel, and after a few tries, it started right up.

During this time, Sherman fished the lake with many local captains, interviewing them and posting his time on Lake Okeechobee all over social media.

Clay and Sherman stood at the same spot, leaning on the boat, three weeks later as Red sat behind the wheel. The new grey carpet sat smooth on the deck. The hull was buffed and waxed and didn't have a scratch on it. The engine, although old, was lubed, oiled and ready for adventure. "I think she's ready," Clay said with a grin on his face. His dad would have been so damn proud of the boat, and of his son.

"The bilge is working, right?" Sherman asked.

"Everything works perfect. Just gotta take her down to the ramp."

"That's gonna be sketchy. I don't trust this thing at all." Sherman kicked the old trailer that the newly restored boat rested upon.

They filled the tires on the old trailer, hooked it up to Sherman's truck, and pulled it out of the garage through the open doors as slowly and gingerly as possible. An ear piercing squeak came from the bearings as they moved for the first time in years. As the boat cleared the open doors and saw sunlight, Clay stopped. "Well, at least we got it out of the barn!" Clay laughed as he sat behind the steering wheel of the boat. "Hop in, buddy!" he said to Red.

With every bump, Clay winced and peered over the side to check on the trailer. He found himself doing the same thing his father did ten years ago, making sure every detail of the boat was in place and correct. Red must've noticed how nervous his dad was to get the thing on the water. "It's right there, dad. We'll get it there."

"A lot can happen between here and there. Shoot, if we get it there and in the water, I'm still not sure the thing will even float. We'll see, I guess."

"It's the moment of truth!" Sherman said as he poked his head out of the driver's window and stopped in front of the ramp.

Clay sat behind the steering wheel, looking behind him and lowering the engine into the water as Sherman backed the trailer in. He cranked the motor, and smoke burst from the exhaust as it fired over but shut off. "Try it again!" Sherman said while filming and driving.

Clay turned the key over once again. This time the engine spit out some smoke and stayed on. "Hahaha!" he laughed as he backed the boat off the trailer. "We ain't sinkin' yet!"

Sherman parked, then held his phone in one hand and three baitcasters in the other as he waddled down the dock and hopped onto the front deck. "She's holding the big man—that's a good sign!" He dropped the rods and gave Red a high five. "Where we headed first?"

"I don't know," Clay said as he leaned back. "The world is our oyster."

"Let's go catch some buoys!" Red said.

"I like the sound of that," Sherman said. "You got a week to figure out how the heck you're supposed to beat me in this tournament."

"Shoot, I ain't worried about you."

"Yeah, not me, huh? Well what about Dirk Wesley?"

Clay looked Sherman dead in the eye. "Dirk Wesley?"

"Who's Dirk Wesley?" Red asked.

Sherman cracked open a soda, crossed his legs, and leaned back. "Go ahead, tell 'em."

"He's one of the best bass fishermen in the world, buddy."

"He's *the* best bass fisherman in the world. I mean, this guy catches 'em wherever he goes. Don't matter."

"And he's gonna fish the tournament next week? The one where there's always at least one drunk that falls off his boat? I don't think this is his kind of fishin'."

"Bingo! That drunk might be me." Sherman paused and looked at Red, who sat with an innocent smile. "Just kiddin', kid. It's not safe to operate boats while under the influence of alcohol." He said it as if it were a legal statement at the end of a pharmaceutical commercial.

Clay and Red just stared at Sherman as they idled through the slow zone, waiting for him to get to the point.

"But... I talked to him last night. I saw he's down here on vacation, stayin' just south of Tampa, couple hours from here. I convinced him to come fish for a nice little warm up before the National Largemouth Series trail starts back up in the spring."

"He seems like a real, excuse my language, Red, asshole," Clay said. "Don't tell your mom I said that."

"He can be hard to get along with sometimes, yes. But my website is bigger than you think," Sherman said with his chest out. "I was one of his first sponsors. Not like he needed the money, his family owns about half of North Carolina. It was more for me—I was just gettin' started too. His success was my success. We had a sym-bi-otic relationship, I guess you could say."

"You still one of his sponsors?" Clay asked as they idled toward open water.

"Hell no. I can't afford him anymore. That's alright though, I got other things goin'."

"Well, that'll be good for the tournament then. Lots of people will come just to see him, I'd imagine."

"Eh," Sherman waved his hand off like he wasn't worried about it. "It'll be a nice surprise. Don't tell anyone. That goes for you, too, Red."

Red shook his head in a very serious fashion.

"It's gonna be great for the tournament. That guy don't go nowhere without a film crew. He's the damn Beyoncé of bass fishin'. "

"It's gonna be good when you beat him!" Red said.

"I just wanna go fishin' with my family. I don't care about beatin' Dirk Wesley or anyone else for that matter. I'm only fishin' this thing to have some fun, and because it was what my pops wanted to do in this boat."

"But you can beat him. Maybe not on any other lake in the country, but you can beat him here. This is your home. You remember where we caught that seven a few weeks back. Home field advantage baby," Sherman said.

"Y'all ready to run?" Clay asked.

"Let her rip son!" Sherman said as he turned his camouflage hat backwards.

Red clung to his seat as Clay pushed the throttle forward and the bow raised in the air. The engine roared and puffed out more smoke, but in seconds the bow lowered, and they were on a plane going thirty-five knots. The boat skidded across the water, and the early fall breeze made the ride nice and cool. Birds flew overhead, and alligators spooked from the thick brush as they rushed by. An intense feeling of being at home, where he belonged, rose over Clay. He eased back the throttle as they entered a large cove surrounded by thick reeds. Bundles of lily pads were scattered throughout the cove, and nickel sized minnows jumped from bushes of hydrilla below the boat. "There's a little bit of everything in here," he said as he looked over the boat and into the water. Red stood next to him, his rod rested on his shoulder like a holstered gun ready to be fired. Sherman didn't move a muscle, just sat at the back of the boat and watched as he drank his soda. As clouds moved in from the north, the temperature dropped, and suddenly, bringing jackets along seemed like it would have been a good idea to all three of them. "Whatcha got rigged up there?" he asked Red, still eyeing the water like a hungry osprey.

"A frog."

"Perfect. Perfect, perfect," Clay said. He was in bass-catching mode.

Red tossed out the dark green frog with a white belly to the edge of a group of lilies. It floated on the surface just as an idle frog might. He twitched his rod and reeled as the frog popped across the water. "Slow it down a tad. And do erratic pops, don't be afraid to stop it for a second in between." Red stopped the frog for a second, then twitched it back and forth two quick times. "Now stop it for a sec."

He put his rod down, and the frog was stationary for a millisecond before there was a wild splash of water and a quick glimpse of a bass as it broke the surface to eat the frog. Overly excited, Red set the hook, but the bass missed the bait, and Red pulled the frog out of the water and almost back to the boat. Sherman giggled in the background. "Hehe. Gotta let 'em eat it, son! That frog can be tricky sometimes. Shoot, I'll still do that time from time."

Red only grunted, then flung the plastic frog toward the same spot. This time it landed in the middle of the lily pads. "That's alright," Clay said. "They'll get up in the lilies too. Reel it slow over the pads, and twitch it when it's in the water."

The plastic frog plopped through the surface and made quite a ruckus of the calm scene. As he let the frog float between two lilies, it looked as if a grenade went off under his bait. Like a wave crashing on the beach, white water sprayed into the air. Red leaned back, but his rod bent the other way, the line stretched from the reel as the lilies parted and a bass thrashed its body out of the water.

Sherman recorded off of his phone in the back of the boat. "Atta boy!"

"That's a real good one!" Clay said as he grabbed the net. "Be easy with her, she's up in the pads."

Red leaned against the bass and pulled it out of the weeds as he reeled as fast as he could. He didn't say anything, only had a fierce look of determination and focus. The head of the bass flailed out of the water and lily pads once again.

"You got 'em now!" Clay said as he dipped the wide net into the water. "It's a good'un!" Red raised his rod over his head to bring the fish to the surface as Clay scooped him up.

"Nice!" Sherman said and stood up.

Red had a big smile across his stunned face. It was a good sized bass, four, maybe five pounds, and had vibrant black markings over it. "That's a damn good start, right there!" Clay said and high-fived his son.

"That's the biggest one I've ever caught," he said, out of breath.

"Hold it up for a picture with your pops!" Sherman said with his phone in his hand. Red picked up the bass by its lip. "Hold that thing out farther! Makes it look bigger that way." Red held it out as far as he could, and Clay stood next to him with the net, like the proud father he was. Sherman got the picture and was content. "Perfect. I'll send that over to ya," Sherman said.

Clay and Sherman sat and watched Red fish for a while. Although, at one point Sherman couldn't stand not fishing and got up and fished next to Red. Clay was happy to sit back, work the trolling motor, and watch his son have a good time just as he and his father once had. Nothing brought him more joy.

CHAPTER 20

FIRST TIME
IN A LONG TIME

Clay's headlights cast long shadows that stretched behind the mobile home. Abi walked through the front door and down the steps as he pulled in front of the house. "Hey, you!" she said as she bent over and gave Red a tight hug. "Did you have fun?"

"Yeah! We finished the boat, then took it out, and I got a buoy!"

Clay stood with his arms crossed and smiled. "A buoy?" Abi asked. "Dang, good job! Say goodnight to your dad and go inside, you have a big day tomorrow."

Abi stepped closer. "How was he?"

"Great, as always. You raised an amazin' kid, Abi."

"Yeah, he is pretty awesome ain't he?"

Abi turned around for a moment to see Red, Bill, and Sue all watching from the living room window. As soon as they realized they'd been caught, they threw the blinds shut. "I'm really glad you and Red have been spendin' time together. I can see a big change in his demeanor. He's been much more confident lately. And just happier."

"He's the one makin' me happier. I'm just tryin' to soak up every second I can with him. You should've seen him on the boat today—he was goin' nuts with me and Sherman."

"I'm glad he's having fun…"

"I would, um… you're more than welcome to come out with us one of these days— that's if you want to."

"I don't know if that's a good idea, Clay."

Clay looked down and shuffled his feet. "Alright, yeah. No problem."

"Maybe it should be just me and you first."

Clay looked up. "Yeah? I would like that."

"How's tomorrow? I don't work."

Clay tried to hide his excitement. "Definitely. Sounds good."

"Okay, cool." Abi walked rather quickly, back up the steps. "I drop off Red at 8:15. I know that's a little late for the morning bite, but would that be okay?"

"Yeah, that's fine. Nine's perfect. Red's gonna be jealous."

"He'll have plenty of time to go fishin'." She smiled and went inside.

Red was still watching through the front window and waved. Clay waved back, happy as could be, and headed home. He couldn't close up shop, but he wasn't going to tell Abi no. So, he called Sherman.

"You miss me already?" Sherman asked as he answered the phone.

"You goin' fishin' tomorrow?"

"Nope, just planned on getting some business stuff done. Why? You want to play hooky from work again?"

"Yes, but not with you."

"Well, that just breaks my heart. Who you goin' with?"

"I'm taking Abi out for a little while. Could you watch over the shop for me?"

"Anything for you bub. Consider it done."

The only button-down shirt that Clay owned hadn't been worn in years, and he had gained a few pounds. It was white with a blue plaid design. He felt like he needed to wear something different and nicer than the same old shirt he wore to church. The wrinkled shirt laid on the pullout bed with a shirtless Clay standing over it. He didn't own an iron. He tried smoothing it out with his hands. That didn't help. He grabbed it by the collar and swished it in the air as if he were opening a trash bag. That didn't help. Feeling use-less—and nervous—he plopped down on the bed. *Should I even wear a collared shirt? I'm going out on the boat.*

Sherman barged into the shop, "Hello? Anybody home?"

"Back here."

Sherman waddled into the doorway. "Why the long face?"

"I don't have a damn iron for this shirt."

"Hmmm." Sherman looked around the room. There was a pan sitting on a single electric stove. "You got a blow torch?"

"What're we gonna do with that? Set the thing on fire?"

"By the looks of it, we should, but no. And I'm not even gonna ask why you're wearing that ugly thing on the boat. You must be nervous as hell. Grab that torch for me."

Clay ran out to the garage, grabbed it, and came back. Sherman stood, spinning the pan in his hand. He dropped his sunglasses over his eyes, grabbed the blow torch, and began heating the bottom of the pan. "That's a good idea, but we could've just used my plug in stove."

Sherman looked like a welder with his sunglasses on as the large flame roasted the bottom of the pan. "Yeah, we could've. But it wouldn't have been nearly as cool." After a minute of heating it up, he took a hook from the desk and poked a small hole in a nearby half drank water bottle, then sprayed the water over the shirt.

"Look at you go."

"And then..." Sherman placed the bottom of the pan on the wet shirt. Steam rolled off the shirt as he moved the pan up and down the shirt just as he would with an iron. "Boom!" he said as he finished the task. "The ol' redneck iron. Works like a champ."

"Thanks, buddy," Clay said as he slipped on the shirt.

"I still don't know why you're wearin' that ugly thing. I wouldn't wear that to dinner, let alone on the boat."

"I wanna look good, that's all."

The chimes from the front door jingled. "Hello?" Abi called out.

Clay tucked in his shirt to his khaki shorts. "Hey," he said as he walked out, Sherman following behind him.

She wore a sundress with a bikini underneath, and Clay thought she looked gorgeous. "Well, hello Abilene," Sherman said as he followed behind Clay.

"Abi, Sherman Puckett. He's an old friend."

"Abi, pleased to meet your acquaintance. I've heard a lot about you. Red and you is all he ever talks about."

"Is that right?"

"Oh yeah, well Clay here can't shut up about yo—"

"Alright, let's get out on the boat, why don't we. Them bass are bitin'. Sherman you got this covered?"

"Yes sir, boss man."

"Alright, call me if you need anything. Are you ready?" he asked Abi.

"Ready when you are."

"Perfect, boat's already in the water waitin' for us. Let's get goin' before Sherman says anything else dumb."

"Oh stop. It was nice meeting you, Sherman."

"Pleasure's mine."

They sat in the boat, and it took a few cranks for the motor to start. "So, we don't have to do anything serious. I figured we could do a little fishin', some cruisin' around. Take it easy," he said as they idled away from the marina.

"I don't know about you, Clay Booker, but I came out here to fish. You can do all the relaxin' you want, but I'm catchin' some bass today."

"Well then, sounds like we're goin' fishin'."

She crossed her legs. "Absolutely." It was silent for a moment. "What in the world are you wearing?"

"What? You don't like it?"

"I do, if we were going out to a fancy steak house or something—not out fishing."

"I just wanted to look nice is all. I guess it is kinda ridiculous, ain't it?"

"It is, but you do look nice."

"Thanks, so do you."

It was silent again. Clay bit his lower lip. "What'd you see in that asshole from the bank?" He told himself he wouldn't bring it up, but there he was, bringing it up already.

Abi laughed. "That didn't take long."

"I mean, I know I ain't all that. But damn, he was a dickhead."

"You're absolutely right. He was."

"God, that bothered me." Clay shook his head as he looked forward into the lake. The chop continued into the horizon as if it were an ocean.

"He was stable, had a good job. And good looking. I was looking for someone to replace you." Clay sat back in the seat. "For a long time, I didn't see anyone. I was hurt, confused, unstable, scared. Scared for Red's future and my own. I even drove by Buoy's a few times over those three years. I always expected to see a big 'For Sale' sign in the front, or maybe just to drive by and see only rubble where you had that whole damn thing demolished. But each time I would slow down, all I would see is a trailer or two from some fisherman, and your old truck. And I knew you were still inside. You hadn't left or burned the place to the ground. You turned into a different person after your father died, just so happened Red was born right after that. There were times those first few years when we lived together that I would see flashes of the Clay I knew before, especially when it was just you, Red, and me. Those flashes showed themselves less and less over the years. But when you came back that Sunday morning, I noticed a spark in your eye that I hadn't seen since you were twenty one years old."

"You mean when you tried to run me over?"

Abi's cheeks turned pink in embarrassment. "Yes, actually. The Clay I had grown to know would've only jumped in front of a car for a bottle of whiskey."

"A bottle of whiskey, sure. But I never quit lovin' you two. I would've jumped in front of a bullet for you two, no matter which Clay you were talkin' about. Somethin' Hank would've never done."

They smiled at each other, and Clay pushed the throttle forward as they took off toward their first spot. They used a spinnerbait and dragged it through the middle of a field of hydrilla. It wasn't fifteen minutes into fishing when Abi ripped the lip of a little bass and giggled as she pulled it out the dark waters of Lake Okeechobee. "Abi, one. Clay, zero."

"Oh man, comin' out with the competition already. You need me to get the hook for you?"

"No sir." She pulled the hook out of the side of the round mouth. "I think I got it."

Then Clay leaned into one that was larger than Abi's, but not by much. He pulled the bass out of the water and up to his chest, then had it dehooked and back swimming again all in thirty seconds. He then cast back out before Abi could make another cast. He grinned as he stared forward. "One, one."

"I see how it's gonna be."

"You started it, I'm gonna finish it."

"Not if I have anything to do with it." She pushed Clay, then cast out herself.

As the day went on, they fished, laughed, and talked about Red. And of course kept score. "How's Red doin' in school?" Clay asked as he cast.

"He's got all A's so far, even after getting suspended over all that nonsense."

"Has he said anything about that bully?"

"Red said the kid doesn't even look his direction anymore."

"Ha! That's my boy."

145

Clay paused for a moment, pointed his rod toward his bait far out in the water, then set the hook. "That's a good'un! What is it now?" he asked while he reeled in the fish. "Eight to seven? I think I'm winning." But then his line went slack and fell to the water.

Abi said nothing, doing the exact motion Clay had just done and laying into a bass. "Yep, that's exactly the score."

He shook his head and chuckled as she pulled in a five pound buoy. Clay didn't say anything, only watched as she pulled up her catch. He thought that was the sexiest thing he had ever seen.

Abi was in first place by lunch. They sat next to each other to eat gas station ham and cheese sandwiches Clay had bought the night before. Abi smirked at the plastic-bound sandwiches cut into two triangles. "Damn grocery store was closed by the time I got there. This was the best thing they had at the convenience store."

"That's alright, I'm so hungry I could eat just about anything right now."

"Cheers." They touched their sandwiches together as if they were beers.

Abi looked down with a grimace as she tried to pretend that the sandwich wasn't disgusting. Clay was thinking the same thing. "Oh, hell," he said with a mouthful, then leaned over the side of the boat and spit.

"Thank God," Abi said, then spit hers out as well. "I didn't want to be rude, but that was horrible."

They laughed and went to take a drink from the water at the same time. Her hand brushed his, and her skin was as soft as Clay remembered. "Oh, sorry. Go ahead."

"Thanks," she said before taking a sip then passing it to him. She smelled like coconut, and her skin was dark and tanned from the morning sun. Her blue eyes shined in the light and were inescapable. Clay couldn't look anywhere else, and neither could she. He leaned in, and so did she, and they kissed for the first time in a long time.

CHAPTER 21

AIN'T NO ONE BETTER THAN ME

A sheet of plywood nailed to a wooden telephone pole at the entrance of a park on the water was spray painted in hand-written white letters that read 'LAKE O EXTRAVAGANZA CAPTAIN'S MEETING'. Red and Clay walked through the parking lot toward the meeting, which was held next to a four way boat ramp in a grass park. They came early, but a few fishermen had beaten them there and were telling stories to one another while sipping drinks. In front of a tent, tables were set up with a long line of foil-covered barbeque waiting to be eaten by the contestants and their families. Inside the tent was a stack of sign-up sheets and a tall golden trophy featuring a bass wrapped around a cowboy boot. A couple named Brent and Dawn ran the tournament.

Clay and Red walked through the park area over to the tent. Red wore a Buoy's Marina, Bait and Tackle hat that matched his father's. Caroline's pink truck bounced through the parking lot. "The Lake O Extravaganza is here, folks!" Sherman declared as he stepped down from the tall truck. "Man, I'm excited!"

"Dear Lord, I can smell that barbeque from here!" Caroline said as she tiptoed in her high-heels and almost rolled her ankle. She had a cocktail in her hand, and it appeared it wasn't her first.

Dawn scrunched her eyebrows together with her hand on her hips. "Who are these folks?" she asked Brent.

"I have no earthly idea, but they ain't from 'round here."

"That's Sherman Puckett," Clay said as he shook his head along with Dawn and Brent.

Sherman whistled through his teeth. "That trophy sure is shiny, ain't it? You can go ahead and give it to me now. We all know who's gonna win this thing," he said as he strutted to the tent. "Look who it is! Them Booker boys are bad news, ain't you heard?" He slapped Red on the shoulder. "Sherman Puckett. Nice to meet ya," he said to Brent.

"Shoot, you don't know half of it," Clay said.

"Brent. How goes it?"

Sherman stepped to the side, distracted by the food. Caroline slapped his hand as he peaked under the aluminum foil that covered mash potatoes. "Get your nasty sausages away from that food." She smiled and hugged Dawn. "Hello darlin', I'm Caroline. Beautiful to meet you. Everything looks delicious. You want a sip? It's vodka. I'm on a diet."

"No, I'm alright. Nice to meet you as well."

"Clay, Red, how goes it gentlemen?" Sherman asked as he filled out the sheet. "You ready to see your dad lose to me tomorrow, Red?"

"He ain't gonna lose!" Red said.

"We'll see what happens. I sure ain't losin' to you. Where's your boy at?" Clay asked.

149

"Who, Dirk? He's just outside of town. He'll be here soon."

"Well, I guess the best bass fisherman in the world don't need to pre-fish."

Soon, more and more people began to gather in the parking lot. Fishermen from all over the lake came to compete in the tournament. It was all smiles from the contestants. Flip-flops, sunglasses, long-sleeved fishing shirts, and chewing tobacco were common among these fishermen. Cowboy hats and tall, gator skin boots were also standard. Diesel trucks rumbled in the background, and there was a loud murmur of fishing talk from all. One man drove up in a swamp buggy with tires that were as tall as Clay. Several conversations continued as the group waited for the meeting to start. Talk of different kinds of bait they'd been using, how fishing's been, and drawn out fishing stories of catching giant fish buzzed around. It was a lighthearted event, and everyone knew each other, and no one took things too seriously—even though they were all great fishermen. Children ran around chasing one another as moms tried their best to keep them in line.

Clay and Red sat at a table with Sherman and Caroline. "Doc, how's it goin'?" Clay asked as an old man approached their table. He had a thin layer of white hair on his head, and his skin was wrinkled and hard like leather. "Good to see ya!"

"Good to see you too, son," he said as he raised his reading glasses, which were hanging from his neck like a necklace, up to his nose. The man struggled to bend over to fill out his information to enter the tournament, but when it came to fishing, he didn't have a problem casting artificials all day.

"How long have you been fishin' this thing?"

"Oh, hell if I know. I can't remember what I had for breakfast this morning. " His hand had a slight shake to it as he wrote. "I'm fishin' this thing till I keel over. I'm just glad to see you here."

"Yeah, I'm happy to be here."

"I heard you're fishin' in your father's rig."

"That I am. Me, Red, and my buddy Sherman here all got it done in a few weeks. She's runnin' like a champ."

"Your dad would be proud," he said as he finished filling out the paper and hung his readers around his neck. "It's been a while since you came in for a checkup, ain't it? You gained some weight, son. Lay off the barbeque, eat a salad."

"Damn, Doc, tell 'em how you really feel!" Sherman said.

Doc chuckled and cleaned his glasses on his shirt. "That goes for you as well, big boy." He patted the table. "Good luck tomorrow, gentlemen. Glad you're back on the water."

"Thanks, Doc." Clay looked down at his watch. It was six fifteen, and it seemed like everyone was there except Dirk Wesley.

Clay leaned back in his chair. "Your boy's late."

Sherman only shrugged and bit into a large piece of brisket. "He'll be here."

"Alright," Brent said and stood up with a microphone in his hand. He tapped it twice, and the single speaker echoed. "This thing on?" The chatter stopped, and everyone turned toward the tent. "What's goin' on, everybody? Welcome to the twentieth annual Lake O Extravaganza." The crowd of a hundred clapped, and there were a few whistles from the back. "For everyone returnin', welcome back, and for any first-time participants out there, just know we don't take things too seriously. We like to have a good time, as most of you already know. I'm real proud of what this thing has turned into over the years. I'm excited to see who takes the trophy. So, uh, I'm done blabberin'. I'll go over the rules real quick and get this out of the way." Brent picked up a piece of paper from the table and squinted as he read. He explained the general rules of the tournament—you must wear a life jacket, one fisherman per boat but another is allowed on the boat, a three thirty check in time, and a five-bass bag each angler gets to weigh.

"You want to come along for the ride?" Clay asked Red.

"Do I get to fish?"

"Nope, you'd have to watch me."

"Then I think I'd rather watch Saturday cartoons."

"Can't blame ya there."

A black SUV with oversized off-road tires parked right next to the crowd, in the middle of the lot. It was pulling an orange bass boat covered in sponsors and decorated with flames traveling from the bow to the stern of the hull. The doors all opened at once, and a full camera crew, already recording, stepped out. They waited for a second as a short, squirrely-looking man walked around the vehicle. He wore a long-sleeved shirt that matched his boat, sponsors and all. He had a mustache, a tight hat, and mirrored sunglasses.

"That's Dirk Wesley," one person in the crowd whispered to a friend. "What the heck is he doin' here?" Everyone was silent; they all knew who he was. Anyone who knew anything about bass fishing knew who he was. "There he is," Sherman said. "Makin' a grand entrance as always."

As he walked through the crowd, the four men followed him. Three of them had professional cameras—the ones that you hold on your shoulder. The other was the sound guy. He held a microphone a foot over Dirk's head as he walked through the crowd. Dirk bumped into Red as he walked through the crowd. "Watch it, kid," he said to Red. Red looked to his dad, who eyed Dirk as he continued on.

He held out his arms like he was greeting an old friend. "The Lake O Extravaganza! Haha, yes! Oh, this is just great. Really, I mean the sign out front and everything. Wow." By this time, he had made it through the crowd and to the tent where Brent stood with the microphone in his hand and a look of annoyance. "I'm here to sign up!"

"Sign-up was twenty minutes ago," he said over the microphone. "I'd be happy to get you signed up after I go over the rules, mister."

Dirk leaned in a little. "Look, you know who I am right?" Brent didn't move a muscle, only looked at him with no expression. "I already know all the rules to these things. Wear your life jacket, don't run no-wake zones, blah blah blah. I'm a busy man with a lot to do. There's no reason for me to sit around here."

"Like I said, sir," Brent said over the microphone once again. "I'll get you signed up in a few minutes. You've shown up late, interrupted the meeting, and now you want all these good people to wait because you have other, more important things to do. Now, please, step aside so we can go on with the rules and everyone can get back to their business."

The crowd was silent, and Dirk turned around to see a grim stare from the audience. He threw up his hands like he was being arrested. "Alright, I get it." He signaled for the cameramen to stop filming, and he stepped aside while

Brent continued with the rules. As soon as he finished, Dirk clapped and stepped back in front of the table. "Let's do this," he said as he rubbed his hands together.

Dawn slid a paper and pen in his direction. "Go ahead and fill all that out for me," she said.

"Can I get an autograph from him, Dad?"

Clay wanted to say, 'no, why would you want an autograph from this asshole?' But he smiled and agreed anyway.

"Yes ma'am!" Dirk said.

Red walked up to him, his cheeks flushed in shyness. Clay watched from behind. "Mr. Wesley, do you think you could sign my hat?"

"Maybe in a little while, kid. I'm busy," he said as he looked down onto the paper.

"He just wants a quick signature, buddy," Clay said.

"What did I say? I'm busy."

Red looked down in embarrassment. "C'mon, Red. Don't mind him." Clay patted his son on the back, and they went for more food.

"How's it goin' Sherman?" he asked his old sponsor as Sherman walked up.

"Dirk, I see you haven't changed a bit."

"I only get better with age, Sherm. I'm like fine wine."

"Hey, buddy," Clay said as he walked up with a plate full of mac and cheese, ribs, and a biscuit. "Clay Booker," he said as he put down his plate.

"I already told ya, I ain't givin' any autographs right now."

"Dirk, this is my good friend, Clay Booker. Y'all met a long time ago, if I remember correctly."

"Hmm. I don't recall. You obviously already know who I am," he said as they shook hands. They shook for longer than normal and looked into each other's eyes. Dirk seemed to be mad, while Clay was calm. Dirk kept squeezing harder every second, but Clay pretended to not notice what he was doing. "Sherman sure has talked you up."

"Yeah, Sherman told me you're a pro. Dirt Weasel I thought it was."

"Ha! That's funny. It's Dirk Wesley. And don't you forget it. Yenno, Sherman said some good things about this tournament, really. He said that whoever wins this is considered the best on Lake Okeechobee. I think he was just pullin' my chain to get me over here, cuz all I see is a bunch of dumb rednecks. I mean c'mon, did he say somethin' about kayaks? I'm about to ed-u-cate all you hillbillies." He stretched out like he was relaxed. "I figured I'd win this thing real quick. Good warm-up for the season."

"We'll see about that," Clay said. "There's a lot of good fishermen in this thing."

"Like who?" he laughed. "I don't see one other guy on the trail. A bunch of nobodies."

"I thought you had a lot to do, Dirt."

"It's Dirk," He hissed. He looked to his film crew, "Start recording." The film crew jumped into action and raised their devices. "This here, folks, is small town fisherman, Clay Booker. He was just asking me for some tips— maybe after the tournament." He held out his hand once again to shake, but Clay kept his hands on his hips, looked down at Dirk's hand then looked away. Dirk slid his hand back, "You have a problem, friend?"

"I ain't your friend, pal."

Dirk slid his tongue across his mustache. "What did you just say to me?"

"Why don't you just go home, little man."

"Little man?" Dirk took a step away from Clay and rolled his shoulders, then fired his fist in the direction of Clay's face. Clay, with his hands still on his hips, moved his body to the side and dodged the blow. Dirk lost his balance and almost fell over.

"Oh, shit," Sherman said and stumbled around for his phone.

Clay clenched his fists, but then noticed how terrified Red was and loosened his grip. Dirk took another swing at Clay, who dodged it again. Then, while Dirk was off balance, Clay pushed him to the ground without much of an effort at all. At this point, the whole crowd was watching, and Dirk's camera crew filming, along with Sherman and many others.

"Quit filming!" he said to his cameramen as he jumped to his feet and adjusted his hat. "I'll see you tomorrow! See how you feel when I put thirty pounds on the board! I'm goin' out there and hammerin' them things tomorrow! Then you'll see, ain't no one better than me!" He hit his chest and put his sunglasses back on, even though it was almost dark out.

"Yeah, we'll see about that."

"Let's get out of this dirt-hole." He strutted back to his SUV with his chest poked out and peeled out of the parking lot like a NASCAR driver leaving the pit.

"Why did you even invite that guy?" Clay asked Sherman.

"He's a bit much, I know."

"A bit much? You saw what just happened, right?"

"He might be fightin' a little bit of Napoleon Syndrome, sure. But he backs it up. Guy is good. Really, really good. And people love him—that's the kind of stuff that gets views. This is going to be great, trust me. After my article and his documentary—or whatever he's doing—come out, and someone else beats him, this will make for great television. I can envision it now—Clay Booker beats the number one fisherman in the world."

CHAPTER 22

LAKE O EXTRAVAGANZA

The scents of freshly brewed coffee and burning gasoline permeated the park as the early morning parking lot was illuminated with red trailer brake lights from the final boats backing down the ramp. Red and green navigation lights floated in the middle of the basin, where boats prepared for takeoff. It was a funny mix of fully rigged bass boats, pontoon boats, trolling-motor-powered bass buggies, kayaks, and even an airboat. The few kayakers waited off to the side of the basin so as to avoid being run over by the boats. Clay jogged over to the tent where Dawn sat behind the table with a large pot of coffee roasting in the humid morning air.

"Mornin', Dawn."

"Goodmornin', honey." She smiled.

"Good luck out there today, Clay!" a man said as he jogged to his boat.

"Hey, you too," he said as he sipped his coffee. "How's everything goin'?"

"Smooth so far. Nobody's backed in to anyone else. There haven't been any fights. Things are goin' well, I'd say."

"Good, good. You see that Dirk Wesley around yet?"

"Yep, he's launched and in the water. Why? Ain't gonna go try to fight him, are ya?"

"Nope, just wonderin'." The final contestant dropped his boat into the water and parked at the end of the lot. "Alright, well I better get goin'. Hope everything runs smooth."

"Good luck, see you later," Clay said.

Brent stood at the end of the dock with a megaphone in his hand. "Five minutes until check out!" He lowered the megaphone. "Good luck out there! Y'all gonna catch some big'uns today. I can feel it!"

"I sure hope so!" Clay said as he jumped in his boat. He turned the key over, and the engine started up, then turned back off again. He turned the key again, and it did the same thing. "Third time's a charm." The third time, the engine rumbled and stayed on. He gave a thumbs up and idled the boat into the group, bumping up next to Sherman.

"There he is!" Sherman said. "That thing turn over for ya?" he asked, talking about the motor.

"She's a little tired this mornin', but I got her goin'."

"Better bring a paddle with you and not go too far from the ramp," Dirk said as he sat low in his seat with one hand on the steering wheel. "I think I'm gonna go ahead and catch my thirty pounds first thing this morning, then go eat a nice breakfast on the water. Maybe crack open a cold one in celebration since you damn near don't win nothin' else in this thing." He looked at his cameraman. "Were you rolling?"

"Yep," one of them said.

"Well, cut that out of the final edit."

"One minute until check out!" Brent yelled from the megaphone. The men whistled and cheered. Clay shook his head and idled forward, away from Dirk. The airboat's engine roared louder than the rest as its long propellers spun as quickly as a helicopter's.

"Good luck, brother!" Sherman said.

"You too, man! I'll see you out there."

"3... 2... 1 go go go!" Brent said over the speaker.

They took off past the marina and into the lake. In a matter of seconds, the pack of vessels was full speed ahead and chasing the sunrise. Clay started at the front, but it was not long before he was in the back, not far ahead of the pontoons. He tapped the throttle as far down as he could. "C'mon, gimme a little more than that!" he said to his motor as if it would respond.

Soon, most of the boats were out of sight and headed in different directions. A streak of bright orange spread across the morning sky, joined by rays of pink and red pointing to the heavens. It was a cool and smooth morning with little wind. The early morning sun reflected off Lake Okeechobee like an abstract painting, with blending colors and long, wavy brush strokes.

Clay was in war mode; he wanted to win. He wanted to win for Red. He also wanted it for himself and his dad. But he especially wanted to beat the conniving Dirk.

His first spot consisted of a long, narrow peninsula that jutted far into the open water. Autumn shad congregated around the point, and the bass waited for an easy meal to swim by. The bass had been blasting them out of the water the last few days. No monsters, just solid three pounders. It was a quick check; if they were there, he would know in a matter of minutes. Birds would be working the shad from the sky, and bass would be chasing them to the surface from below. As he turned south and ran down a line of reeds, he looked ahead and squinted. The reeds cut far out into open water, and that was the point he wanted to check. He didn't see any birds working the point, which was not a good sign. "Shoot," he said to himself as he idled forward. Without wasting a single second, he turned off the motor and swiped a rod that was rigged with a soft-body swimbait that resembled a shad. He dropped the trolling motor into the water and began scanning the water like a hawk. He looked each and every direction, then up in the sky for birds again. Nothing. He didn't even make a cast. "Shoot," he repeated as he jumped behind the steering wheel. *The birds are better fisherman than you or I will ever be*, his father used to say. *Follow the birds, and you will find the fish.* "On to the next one."

Sherman headed northeast to a shallow marsh area scattered with deep ditches. During the fall, the shad liked to congregate in those deeper ditches. Sherman had been catching some decent sized fish there, but they weren't going to win him the tournament. He had other spots he wanted to fish first, but the guides he had been fishing with were all in the tournament, and those were their spots. After all, he was there to make connections—and ultimately fans of his website. The last thing he wanted to do was piss off the mighty Bubba Lox. Sherman was afraid of that boulder of a man. There was no need to step on any toes. After all, fishermen don't take other fishermen's spots, especially during a tournament.

Before he stopped to fish, he adjusted the camera that was attached to his console. It would be recording all day. Eight rods were strapped to the gunnels, all rigged for different situations. He picked a bright green worm with a weedless hook attached to a Carolina rig for his first bait of choice as he slowed to the edge of a ditch. He had to trim his motor up because it dragged the muddy bottom.

Before he came down to Lake Okeechobee and became friends with Clay again, he hadn't used a Carolina rig since he was a kid. He knew it caught fish, but it was an old-school method of bass fishing, and he got caught up in the flashy new lures and ultra-realistic baits. He'd made fun of Clay the first time he pulled it out a few days ago while they were pre-fishing. He quit after Clay pulled three bass in a row out of a hole. Then Sherman switched over to it as well.

His boat tilted back and forth as he stepped onto the front casting deck. His breath was heavy as he slung the Carolina rig sideways to the deep cutout. He dragged the worm across the bottom, but he didn't see much action at the surface. Then again, he never did when he fished here. There was nothing the first thirty minutes he was there as he ran the trolling motor up and down the edge of the deep. He stopped four different times to switch worms. After the bright green, he tried a dark speckled green, then purple, then a blue speckled. Two more ditches were ahead of him, but this was the one he had caught most of his fish in. "One more cast."

Again, he slung out, now with his blue speckled worm. He dragged his rod sideways, rested and reeled the slack, pulled it, reeled, pulled, then he felt just the slightest difference at the end of his line. It began to move sideways across the water, he reeled up the slack and set the hook. "There he is!" he said as if someone else stood on the boat. "Oh, that's a good'un… oh, that's a good'un." He exhaled like he was lifting a heavy weight as he pulled the fish in. With one hand, he held the rod, and with the other, he grabbed his net, then dipped it far out into the water as he pulled the fish in. "Woooo!" he yelled as he held the bass up by the lip. It was a healthy fish, with a big belly from munching on shad. "That's a fatty right there! Or as Clay Booker says, that's a BUOY!"

Dirk continued to run his boat as others fished. He hadn't done any pre-fishing, but he didn't have to. He was Dirk Wesley, the best bass fisherman in the world. However, that wasn't why he didn't need to pre-fish. He had some sort of connection in every major lake in the United States, and Lake Okeechobee was no different.

He'd made a few phone calls to guides on the trip over from the west coast of Florida, asking where the fish have been, what he should use—all the details he needed to know to win the tournament. The first two guides he called hung up on him for two reasons: they were fishing the tournament, and they didn't like Dirk. The third phone call proved to be a helpful one. A young man named Fred, who had become a captain a few months before, was eager to talk to Dirk and tell him whatever he needed. Fred told him that about fifteen miles south of the tournament, there were monsters being caught on spinnerbaits. That was a perfect combination for Dirk; fishing spinnerbaits allowed him to fish fast and cover a lot of ground until he keyed in on the real hammers. There was nothing else for him to go off, so that was his plan. Plus, he could figure things out on the water and adjust as he fished. He told Fred to not tell anyone of their talk, and that he would fish with him soon. Dirk knew that was a lie, but he couldn't have people knowing he was asking other anglers where to fish and what to use.

The cameramen sat next to him, filming the entire time. He rushed down the shoreline, passing boats only feet away, leaving them in his wake, and spooking any fish that may have been around them. "Don't show any of that!" he said over the wind as he sped down.

As he made it to the area Fred had described, a malicious grin appeared on his face. Similar to Clay's spot, a thick peninsula jutted from the mainland, and at the end of this peninsula was a cove-like cutout with many points where the reeds receded and then jutted back out. Several ospreys circled the cove from the air, along with seagulls trying to steal a meal from the sky. "Don't just look at me! Don't you have enough footage of me?" he said to one of the cameramen and threw his hand up as he idled to the spot. "Look at all that! That's what you need to be filmin'! I know I'm good lookin', but damn."

"They're getting all of that," the head cameraman said about the other two cameramen.

"Now, boy, don't question me. I'm payin' you, aren't I?"

"Yes, you are."

"Well then, that makes me your boss, and what I say goes."

"But they—"

Dirk's face began to turn red. "I said it once, and I won't say it again! Get that shot!"

By this point, the other men had stopped what they were doing to watch. "Yes sir," he said, and turned with an aggravated look.

"What the hell are y'all lookin' at?" Dirk asked the other men as they staired. They said nothing, only turned back to their cameras. He snatched three rods from under the gunnel. "Sheesh, can't get any good workers nowadays."

The birds flew overhead and dove into the water around them, hoping to come out with a shad for breakfast. Dirk made his first cast with a golden spinnerbait and a nat-ural-colored soft plastic that resembled a small bait fish. He reeled at a constant speed and pulled the bait through thick patches of hydrilla that grew below the surface. "There's one," he grunted as he set the hook. It was small, and the bass skipped along the water as he quickly reeled it in. "Just a baby," he said as he lifted it up out of the water. "He ain't gonna make the cut."

The engine rumbled as Clay idled into his next spot, which was a short ride away. A thick growth of pennywort looked like bright green matts floating on the surface—Red senior used to call them money mats. There were hundreds of these mats that stretched a mile to shore. Clay had come across the money mats two days earlier on an evening trip after work. He hadn't caught anything on them, but they looked fishy, like a monster Largemouth could strike any second. Since he was close by, he thought he'd check them again. No birds patrolled the air, but that didn't mean the fish weren't there. Bait liked to get under those mats for protection from the predators above and below. He leaped from behind the wheel onto the deck, ready to find monsters.

Wasting no time, he cast before he got to the first mat. And then again, and again, and again. As he got into the thick, he zigzagged his way in and around the clouds of vegetation with the trolling motor. He swam his weedless bait through the channels on the edge of the mats but was unsuccessful the first few minutes there. He knew he needed bass in the boat soon. He switched rods to a purple beaver with a punching skirt on it since it would get through the thick stuff. He zoomed closer to a mat and began flipping his weighted plastic onto it. The weight was pointed and fell through the thick brush with no problem. This was a painstakingly slow type of fishing when they weren't biting, but it was a good way to catch those tournament winners. Clay knew that when he got on them good, it was a fun type of bite, so he circled one mat at a time and made sure to drop the purple beaver in every little opening he could.

His confidence was lost after an hour with no bites and hundreds of flips. He was looking off into the distance as he flipped his bait into another thick mat, not paying attention, when the line took off and the rod began to slip from his grip. Startled, he set the hook, and it was as if he'd hooked a boulder that fought back. There was none of the give he'd expect from a smaller bass. His rod bent over, and lined peeled in the opposite direction, through the thick. "Holy shit!" he said as he tried to fight the fish and control the trolling motor at the same time. The bass pulled him into the thick weed, and he knew it could easily break off or spit the hook with all the grass stuck on his line. Clay put the trolling motor into full throttle in the middle of the thick money mat, right over the top of the monster below. He dropped to his stomach like he was about to perform a push up. Pennywort splattered onto the deck as he pulled the braided line in with his hand. He could feel the stubborn brute on the other end giving all it had to not to be captured. It was a battle between man and bass.

But, suddenly, the bass switched direction as he pulled off the last of the pennywort from the line, and it burst from the water like a great white chasing a seal off the South African coast. Clay jumped to a knee and saw it like it was in slow motion—the monstrous fish emerged from the shadows and shook its massive head while it was airborne. With one major shake of the head, the hook flew from its mouth and toward his face. Clay grunted in pain. The hook had buried its barb deep into Clay's left cheek.

"You gotta be kiddin' me," he mumbled with a lisp. He felt the inside of his cheek with his tongue and winced in pain. The hook stuck into his mouth through his cheek. Blood dripped from his purple, swollen face onto the deck of the boat. Just grabbing the hook sent pain racing through his face. He took a few deep breaths, closed his eyes and tried to pull the hook out, but the agony was too great, and he had to stop. The hook had not moved. In a state of frantic helplessness, he rummaged through his tackle bag in search of pliers. *If only I would've hooked that bass as good as I damn hooked myself,* he thought. Finally, he found his set of pliers at the bottom of the bag and gripped the side of the boat because he knew that this was not going to be an easy—or painless—process.

"C'mon," he said as he lifted the pliers with an unsteady hand up to his cheek. He shut his eyes and winced as the pliers took hold of the hook. He clenched his teeth, and pain shot throughout his face as he pulled on the hook. "Shit!" His breaths were deep and short as he tried again, but the hook didn't budge. He didn't have time for this. He needed to be fishing; time ate away at the clock, and each second he wasn't fishing was a second where others fished ahead of him. He pulled again, harder this time. His cheek stretched as he pulled, and he groaned in pain. Then it popped out. He threw the pliers, still clenching the hook, onto the deck as he held his cheek. The taste of iron permeated his mouth, and he spit blood into the water. The palm of his hand was red as he wiped his cheek. A streak of blood stained the butt of his fishing rod as he stepped back onto the front deck and got back after it.

The sun was high in the sky, and Sherman's shirt was drenched in sweat even though it was a beautiful, cool, fall day. He sat behind the wheel with his feet propped up on the deck, eating a sandwich.

He sighed happily as he leaned farther back in his seat and stared at the clouds with a smile. There was a small dash camera attached to his console that he picked up and held with both hands like he was going to take a selfie. Like a lion tearing its meat from the bone, he snatched a mouthful of his sandwich as he recorded himself. "Here we are folks—Lake Okeechobee, high noon. I'm fishin' the Lake O Extravaganza. My good friend Clay Booker told me about it, and I had to get in on the competition. Some of the best guides on the lake fish this thing every year, so I thought I'd come down and give it a try myself." Crumbs of bread and turkey fell from his mouth as he spoke. "Well, I'd say I've done pretty darn good this mornin'." He chuckled to himself as he leaned over to his livewell and put the camera close to the water. "You see them chunks? There's twenty-two pounds floatin' around in that there livewell." He turned the camera back to his face. "I'd like to see anyone beat that. I'm feelin' real confident. I'm sittin' pretty. I think I might just work on my tan the rest of the day. Tune back in to see that big gold trophy I'm gonna be holdin' up later today." He pointed his pudgy finger at the camera. "And if you haven't already, like and subscribe to The Alabama Largemouth on all platforms!"

"Hahaha! That's what I'm talkin' about right there!" Dirk pumped his fist back and forth in the air as he held a fat bass up to the camera. He ran to the back of the boat, pushing one of the cameramen out of the way in the process. As he attached the scale to the bass's gill, digital numbers bounced around until they stopped at five point four pounds. "Yes! That's what I needed! Yes, yes, yes!" With a balled fist, he pounded his chest multiple times, then dropped the bass into his livewell. In the tank, four good ones swam, and with that fish, he had twenty-five pounds in the boat. "Woo!" he said as he raised his hand to high-five one of the cameramen. The man flinched at first, but then gave him a high five while still filming.

"That's what I needed," he said, out of breath, as he picked his rod up and began fishing again. "Been lookin' for that big bite all day, and I found it on the spinnerbait. That's what separates the good from the great," he said as he cast. "The good would be happy with twenty pounds in the livewell like I had. Nope. Not me. I demand greatness at all times, that's what separates me from the rest. That's why I'm numero uno."

Clay took a sip of water as he peered into his livewell, he had about fifteen pounds altogether. A respectable weight, but he knew that wasn't going to get him anywhere close to winning. His entire face burned with pain, and he could feel the swelling increase by the minute. Over and over he played out what he could've done differently to land that monster that got away. He shook his head in disappointment, which sparked more pain. It was two thirty, and he had finished fishing his last spot. He didn't have any spots in the back of his head he could try until the three thirty check-in time. He was about a twenty minute ride back to the marina and considered calling it quits and going in. "No," he said. "That's not what Dad would've done. He would've fished until the very last minute he could. I got time."

Clay revved the engine, but it didn't start. He revved it again, and it gurgled for a second, then turned off. "C'mon…" He tried one more time, and it started. The engine kicked up sediment into a puff of brown mud as he idled his way into deeper water toward the middle of the lake. He looked left, then right. At this point, it seemed impossible to find the winners; he was all out of ideas. The only logical thing to do, outside of going back in early, was to fish his way back to the boat ramp.

He began to turn the steering wheel as two low flying ospreys soared past him like fighter jets on a mission. He watched as they continued toward the middle of the lake, where there was nothing but open water as if it were a brown water ocean. "That's weird…" He continued idling in the direction of the marina. They kept flying at an incredible pace until they were almost out of sight, and then they seemed to stop. At that point, they were like small grey dots in the sky, but those grey dots hovered over one spot and dove into the water. Still not convinced he needed to investigate, he pushed the throttle forward, but as the bow raised, another osprey flew overhead toward the others. He turned the steering wheel hard to the left toward open water. *I got nothin' to lose.*

The bow lowered as the boat skidded the surface toward the tiny grey dots circling the sky. Clay's hair began to fly backward as he took off his hat before it flew off. His heart beat increased as he grew closer to the ospreys. He had that tingling feel in the tips of his fingers and toes, a feeling that he had blindly run into some good fishing.

He slowed to an idle as ospreys, seagulls, and white pelicans dove into the water in front of him. A football field length of thick shad flipped in front of him. The birds gawked from above, and seagulls fought each other over fish. This is what he had been looking for all day. It was absolute chaos. His palms sweat as he ran to the deck; he had an hour to fish. His first cast with a Gambler big EZ swim bait hooked a dinker, one less than two pounds. Then he caught another dinker, and another.

"Well this is fun, at least," he said as he threw the little guy back into the water. Now he only had thirty minutes of fishing left before he had to leave, with no upgrades in his well. Clay felt confident he had time to find a larger bass than those he already had.

With the trolling motor, he moved to the outside of the shad. Maybe the bigger ones were sitting in the shadows waiting for an easy meal. He cast, and before he could reel once, his line went slack, but he didn't feel anything. He reeled in the slack as quickly as he could, and as it came tight, it felt like a mossy jawed brick was on the end of his line. This thing was a thumper. His heart beat out of his chest as the fish refused to give an inch. It stayed down, never jumped once. It peeled out line, but Clay was able to drag him in with finesse. "That's what I'm talkin' about!" He leaned over the side of the boat and lipped the bass with his thumb. It looked to be over five pounds, but he didn't have time to weigh it. He dropped it in the well and kept fishing.

A few casts later, boom! Another big hook up. This one felt just as big or bigger than the last, "Nice, nice!" He dropped to his stomach and pulled it out of the water. It was shorter than the last but had a protruding belly filled with shad from stuffing its face. This time, he took out the two smallest bass in the well, then dropped the big boy in with his friend. He wanted to weigh the five heaviest he could catch. Racing against the clock, he cast back out before he even made it to the front of the boat. It was another automatic hookup, and this one wasn't budging from the bottom. It dragged the line out, then when Clay gained some ground, it dragged line out again. "Thing is fightin' like a tuna," he said as he put pressure on the fish to get him in. "C'mon… c'mon." The fish was close to the boat. As it came within reaching distance, he fell down to his stomach and the monster jumped right next to the boat. Its mouth could've fit a football in it, and Clay's swim bait looked like a peanut compared to the fish. As it flared back and forth, he was able to get a thumb into its lip and pull him in. "Yes sir! Yes sir!" His heart was racing. This one was as fat as the other, but much longer. "I can't believe it. That thing is seven plus, I guarantee it." He was panting. He checked the time, fifteen minutes until check in was over.

Shad flipped all around him still, and the birds dove like crazy. There were more big bass to be caught, but his time was up. He needed to leave now if he wanted to get back before the cut off time. He slammed the well hatch closed and fell behind the wheel. As he turned the key, the motor didn't turn over for a second. He tried again, and a high-pitched screech, like nails on a chalkboard, sounded from the insides of the engine. "Shit," he said as he looked back at the engine. "C'mon, ol' gal." He turned the key over once again, and the same screech echoed over the lake. It was three twenty. "Shit!"

As birds dove onto the bait fish around him, he rolled to the back of the boat and ripped the cowling off the motor to inspect the issue. At first glance, he could see nothing wrong except that it was an old motor that needed more work done to it. "Hmm…" While studying each dynamic of the motor, he tried to turn the key over again and saw the issue. He looked at his watch, 3:22.

A screw was loose between two rotating parts and was scratching the metal next to it. He didn't have a screwdriver in the boat, so he tightened it the best he could with his fingers and hoped for the best. Again, he turned the key, and the motor rumbled on. "Yes! Alright..." he said, thinking aloud. "Cowling on... let's go." Before he could fully sit down, he pushed the throttle as far forward as it could go. It was 3:24.

CHAPTER 23

OKEECHOBEE HEAT

A humorous mixture of glimmering bass boats, pontoons, bass buggies, and an airboat docked on the shoreline of the park. Red paced back and forth at the end of the ramp beside the shoreline where the boats were parked, waiting for his dad with Abi. Every boat was in except for Clay's and Dirk's. Sherman was the first one back and claimed he was going to be the big winner. It was 3:25, and there was no sign of either of them.

A stage big enough to be used for a small concert was set up in the well-manicured grass. On the side of the stage, fishermen lined up with their bags filled with water and what they hoped were the winning fish while friends and family waited for the weigh in. Abi checked the clock; it was now 3:26. "Alright, everyone is hungry and needs a beer, including me," Dawn said into the microphone on stage. "Let's get this thing going. First up, Sherman Puckett!"

With his nylon bag filled with water and five bass, Sherman waddled onto the stage, a big grin on his face. People clapped, but the loudest from the crowd was Caroline, who raised her cocktail to the sky and cheered over the murmur of the crowd. "That's my baby, right there!"

"Show us your two big fish, Sherman," Dawn said into a microphone. Held by their lips, Sherman raised his two largest fish. "Those are lookin' good. Let's get that weight." He placed each of the fish onto the water scale, "Twenty-one point eight pounds. That's a good weight, Mr. Puckett. Alright up next we have Bill—"

Sherman leaned over into the microphone. "I'd just like to say real quick that if y'all like bass fishin', go check-out my website," he raised his fingers in the sky like he was making quotes, "The Alabama Largemouth dot com. I do all sorts of stuff—podcasts, videos—"

"Alright! Thank you, Sherman!"

It was 3:28, and in the distance Red saw a boat flying toward the marina at full speed. In a matter of seconds, it was close enough to see that it was Dirk, and Red's heart dropped. The orange hull reflected the sunlight and blinded Red as Dirk came to a screeching halt two minutes before the cut off time. With a timid look, Red apprehensively raised his hand in the air as a kind gesture. The cameramen waved back, but Dirk did not. Then, around the corner came Clay, with seconds to spare.

"That was close!" Red said through cupped hands.

Clay threw up his hands as he approached the shore-line. "I couldn't get the dang engine started!" As he parked on shore, he filled his bag with his five bass and jumped onto land.

"What happened to your face?" Red asked.

"Clay!" Abi gasped and snatched his glasses off his face. The wound dribbled a single drop of blood down his plum purple cheek. But then she ran her fingers over his face, and the touch soothed any pain he had. "You need stitches."

175

"I'll be fine, hook smacked me in the face. Had to pull it out with pliers like I was a damn bass. Guess they got their revenge on me."

"Wow! Cool!"

"Redmond! Not cool!"

"You got any buoys in there?" Red asked as he peeked in Clay's bag filled with his five bass and the water to keep them alive.

Clay grinned. "I got a couple good'uns."

"How big are they?"

"Well, let's go and find out, why don't we."

Dirk stood in front of him as the line continued to move forward onto the stage. He flinched as he took a look at Clay. "Jesus. What, did a gator get ya?"

"Hook."

Dirk shook his head. "Hope you hooked as many bass as you hooked yourself. Have a little athleticism out there. On the tournament trail, some rookie usually gets popped with a jig. Not me though." He moved his body side to side as if he were blocking punches that Clay wished he could throw. "I'm quick as lightin'."

"Let's let the scale do the talkin', bubba."

"Shit." Dirk spit onto the ground in front of Clay's shoes. "I don't think you want that." In the most conceited way possible, he leaned to one side with the bag of fish in his hand as if he were carrying a hundred pounds. "This is one heavy bag I got here. I couldn't imagine what I would have done if I pre-fished."

Clay paid no attention to him, instead waving at Abi and Red, who'd found Sherman and Caroline in the crowd and were watching Dawn call out weights as each angler took the stage with their bass. When Clay was a kid, not much older than Red, his dad would take him to this weigh-in every year. He'd longed to be one of those anglers taking the stage, sunburnt and tired from a full day on the water, but proud to present their catch to the crowd. "I'm gonna win this thing one day," Clay would say to his dad, and his dad would always respond, "Not if you're fishin' against me."

The murmur from the crowd said it was a great day for everyone. A lot of fish were caught, and the bite was hot. Between anglers, Abi and Clay made eye contact, and she scrunched her eyebrows together and smiled at him.

"Next we have Dirk Wesley. C'mon to the stage Dirk," Dawn said. "You need twenty-five pounds to win it, Dirk. You think you got that?"

"Oh yes, ma'am, I most definitely have that. It was a real fun day out there, and I'm glad I could come out and compete against such great fishermen all day."

"Alright, let's find out." He dropped his fish into the water scale, and the digital numbers climbed. "Twenty-six point two pounds! We have a new leader!"

Dirk licked his mustache with his hands on his hips as he leaned to one side. "That sounds about right. I think your scale's a little light, but that's alright."

Dawn rolled her eyes and patted him on the back. "Alright folks, last but not least, we have Clay Booker."

Sherman whistled through his teeth from the back of the small crowd. Clay waved at Red and Abi as he took the stage. "You have a steep weight to go up against, Clay. That better be a heavy bag you got right there. Can you pull off some last minute heroics?"

"I think it's gonna be real close."

"Then let's find out, drop 'em on in the tank."

Clay dropped the five bass into the tank. The big ones flopped in last and floated at the top for a moment longer than the smaller ones, just as if they were actual buoys. The numbers on the scale sky rocketed, then slowed as they reached the mid-twenties. Clay watched the numbers as they seemed to move in slow motion. Twenty-five point zero... Twenty-five point eight... twenty-six point two... twenty-six point six... twenty-seven even. The numbers halted. Red jumped up and down with his hands in the air. Clay's heart skipped once, and the first thought that came to mind was not that he beat Dirk Wesley or won the trophy, but the image of shit-eating grin his father would have had to see his son win the Lake O Extravaganza in his own boat.

"And Clay Booker comes in at the last second with twenty-seven pounds, ladies and gentlemen! Wow!"

Dirk threw his hands in the air and signaled for his cameramen to turn off the cameras. As the crowd waited for Dawn and Brent to gather the tournament prizes, Clay made his way off stage with long, confident strides. He intercepted Dirk as it seemed like he was headed back to his boat.

"Hey bud, just wanted to tell ya thanks for comin' out. It was a pleasure to fish against you. Hope there's no hard feelin's between us." Clay put his hand out for a shake, but Dirk only spit on the ground in front of him.

"Congratulations, you can find bass on one lake. You think that impresses me or somethin'? Jesus, man, I mean, look around. There are freakin' kayaks in this thing. Congratulations, you're the king of the clowns. Go grind out a week on a lake you've never been on against the best fishermen in the world, out in the elements. Wind, rain, sleet, snow... doesn't matter. I'm out there catchin' 'em day in and day out."

"Apparently, today it did matter. Maybe you can't handle the Okeechobee heat."

Dirk shook his head. "You wouldn't last a second on the trail."

"We'll see about that."

"This guy thinks he can compete with me, what a joke." He turned to his cameramen. "Let's get the hell out of this piece of trash town. Smells like cow shit wherever you go. I can't stand it."

"Okay, folks. It's time for what everyone has been waiting for! I'd like to thank each and every one of you for coming out and fishing. From what I've heard, it was an awesome day out there! I'm just glad all of the anglers got back safely for yet another Lake O Extravaganza. Alright, without further ado, in third place, with twenty-four point nine pounds, Bubba Lox! C'mon up, Bubba!" The mountain of a man made his way to the stage and towered over Dawn. He took his rod and reel combo that looked like a child's toy in his hands and retreated back to the crowd. "Next up, coming in second place, I'm sure most of you know him already, Dirk Wesley!" The crowd clapped, but Dirk was a no show. "Looks like we'll have to send Dirk his prizes, I guess. Aaand the moment we've all been waiting for... this year's Lake O Extravaganza champion... In first place, with twenty-seven pounds, Clay Booker!"

Clay proudly ran up to the stage. Red cheered from the front of the crowd, and Clay leaned over and gave him a high five as Dawn gave Clay the trophy. "Looks like those battle scars paid off for you Clay!"

"Shoot, I'd take a hook to the face any day of the week to win. My pops always wanted to come fish this thing, and he never got the chance. Just glad I could take it home for him."

"Alright! Great job, Clay! Thank you all for another great bass-fishin' extravaganza. I'm so happy you all could come. Please hangout for as long as you'd like. We have plenty of refreshments as most of you have already found." Just as quickly as it began, the Lake O Extravaganza was over.

"Look at the black-eyed champ!" Sherman said. "Twenty-seven pounds." Sherman whistled through his teeth. "That's a damn good day. I bet you could make some big money doin' this."

Clay laughed. "Yeah, I could win the lottery as well."

"You just beat the number one bass fisherman in the world after not fishing for all this time. Clay, you could be the best to ever do it."

Sherman and Caroline had their bags packed and ready to head back to Alabama the day after the Lake O Extravaganza. Before they left town, their jacked-up diesel trucks rumbled into the parking lot of Clay's shop. Sherman engulfed Clay with a big hug. "It's been fun, don't be a stranger, now. Y'all gotta come up to 'bama real soon to do some fishin'."

"I'm gonna miss y'all so much!" Caroline said with tears in her eyes. She hugged Abi, who was at the bait shop with Red and Clay. She had only met Caroline a handful of times now and was surprised at the affection. Abi assumed she had started drinking before the drive. Caroline grabbed Red and pulled him in as well, "Don't be shy, Redmond, we're practically family now."

"We'll make our way up, maybe when Red gets out of school this summer," Clay said.

"It better be earlier than that!" Sherman demanded. "Our early winter bass bite is epic, I'm tellin' ya. It can get a little chilly, but it sure is fun. We ain't too far from the coast either. We can go get on the redfish bite down in the gulf."

"We got a nice guest house, too. Red can sleep on our pull out so you two can have your alone time," Caroline said to Abi with an over-exaggerated wink.

Red looked confused. "We'll see about that," Abi said.

"Just a fair warning, I plan on mentioning you around the website," Sherman said. "Just because I'm of course gonna talk about the tournament and all. Gotta give credit where credit is due."

"Yeah sure, do whatever you want, buddy," Clay said.

Caroline rolled her eyes. "Oh hell, don't tell him that. Sherman has had all sorts of wild ideas since the tournament. Those bass you caught really got him thinkin'."

CHAPTER 24

MISTER BUOY

Lazy eyed, Clay sipped on his coffee as he listened to bluegrass on the radio and slipped on his flip flops. The cool fall air swirled through an open window and was a nice change from the brutal summer heat that was now a thing of the past. The Lake O trophy glistened in the corner of the dim room next to a picture of him and Red fishing on the pond behind the church.

With autumn in full force, he figured there might be a boat or two launching at the marina, but nothing crazy. The marina was never too hectic. He heard a honk, and then another as he walked out of his room and into the shop. "What the…" he said to himself as he turned down his music. Trucks with trailered boats lined back into the road. He peered through the blinds; multiple red brake lights glowed around the parking lot, which was already full. "What is goin' on?"

People stood outside their trucks, conversing with one another as they tied on different baits and readied their boats for the day ahead as they awaited their turn to launch. There were more than just bass boats. Saltwater bay boats and flats boats waited in line. He didn't recognize anyone. Clay's keys jingled as he unlocked the front door and took a step outside. Still with sleep in his eyes and bed hair, he sipped on his coffee as he watched the scene unfold in front of him.

One man asked, "Where the buoys bitin' today, Clay?" as he tied on a topwater frog.

"You're the man, Clay!" another man said from his truck.

Clay waved, confused. He closed the door to the shop behind him and turned on the lights. The shop wasn't supposed to open for another thirty minutes, and he usually watched the news and drank his coffee before opening, but Clay had never seen that many people using the ramp before. His phone vibrated in his pocket over and over again. He didn't have a personal social media account, but he did run one for Buoy's Marina, Bait and Tackle, which he rarely posted on. Hundreds of notifications popped up on his phone. He had text messages from people he hadn't talked to in years. "What is goin' on?" he asked himself once again while rubbing the sleep from his eyes.

He lifted a single blind at the window behind the counter, as if he was spying on a neighbor and didn't want to be seen. His phone continued to vibrate with notifications, and he finally picked it up to investigate. The first text was from Sherman at seven last night, long after Clay had put his phone down for the night.

Sherman: Just put out everythin, don't be surprised if ur busy tmrrw

At the end of the message was a link to his website. "Sherman, what did you do…"

Clay skimmed through the article, which featured pictures of him and Red holding up big bass on his boat. There was a faint smile on his face, not because he was included

183

in Sherman's work, but because Red was going to be excited about being included. He peered through the blinds once again as trucks backed their boats down the ramp.

A man with a thick goatee that hung well below his chin opened up the door shyly and stuck his head in. "You open, man?" he asked in a southern accent.

Clay pulled the chain to the neon OPEN sign hanging in the window, "Now I am, come on in."

The man strolled up and down the aisle like he was in a grocery store, grabbing each thing that sparked his interest. "I always use the public ramp a few miles down, but shoot, I had to come check this place out after you beat that Dirk Wesley." He whistled through his teeth. "You might not get that lucky ever again."

"Lucky?"

The next thing Clay knew, another fisherman walked in, then two young parents and a kid, and two more fishermen after that. It was crowded in the cramped tackle shop. Clay had never had this problem before. He ran bag after bag of soft plastics, hooks, weights, topwaters, creature baits, beaver tails, everything on the walls.

"MmmMmmMmm!" a plump man hummed as he rubbed his beer belly while awaiting checkout. "I'm buyin' baits from a local superstar. If I could just get one of those fish you caught in that tournament while I'm fishin' today, I'd be a happy camper. What'd you call 'em again? Buoys?"

"Yeah, that's right. It was somethin' me and my dad came up with a long time ago," Clay said as he stuffed a paper bag with miscellaneous tackle items. "It's kinda became a local sayin', I guess."

"Well, it ain't local anymore." The man chuckled as he grabbed his bag. "You need to ditch this place and get on the pro tour," he said as he walked out the door.

"You really beat Dirk Wesley?" a kid asked, standing on his tippy toes to look over the counter and placing two bobbers down. His parents stood behind him and grinned at their son.

"I did, buddy."

"Kent here is a big fan of all things bass fishing," his mother said as she held her hand on her son's shoulder. "He watches all sorts of fishing videos on the internet."

"That's all he watches," the dad said. "And I couldn't be prouder."

"That's great, little man, keep fishin'. Don't take years off like I did."

"Could I get your autograph, Mister Buoy?" the boy asked with a sparkle in his eye.

"Oh," the mom chuckled, "he's too busy for that."

Clay was surprised. "It's fine, sure I will. What would you like me to sign, buddy?"

Kent took off his hat. "Right here, please," he said, pointing to the underside of his bill. "You're gonna be world champ one day. I just know it."

"I don't know about all that," Clay said as he scribbled his name on the bill. "But thanks for the confidence, little man."

"Thanks, Mister Buoy," Kent said as he put his hat back on and held out his tiny fist for a bump. His parents just stared at their son in amazement, and Clay laughed as he bumped fists with his new fan.

As the morning continued, more and more people piled into the shop. Soon, the shelves were barren, and Clay needed to restock. Once the line of boats were off and into the water, and the sun rose into the sky, he was able to take a breath and think about what had just happened. He smiled and laughed to himself; he had never seen it this busy before. He called Sherman.

"Mr. Booker! Miss me already?" Sherman asked over the phone.

"What in the hell did you put in that article, man? I had a line of fifty boats wanting to get in here this mornin'." Clay peeked out the window. "It looked like the damn National Largemouth Series had a tournament goin'. There ain't a single space open. Trucks are all parked on the side of the road. It's damn chaos, is what it is."

Sherman chuckled. "I told you I got push, brother. I may have mentioned you a time or two in the blog. And in the video, and podcast. People love an underdog story."

"I mean, this is crazy. You should see my shelves, ain't nothin' left. I gotta order all new stuff."

"That's a great problem to have, my friend."

"I don't know how you did it, but I can't thank you enough, Sherm."

"Ah, shut up with all that."

"I'm serious man, ever since you came down, things have been goin' great. With this many people comin' around, I'll be sittin' pretty here real soon. I owe you."

"Only thing I ask is when you make it big on the pro tour, you don't forget about little ol' Sherman."

"I'd love to, I really would. But I don't have the capital, the sponsors, and I don't think I can be away from Red and Abi that long. I've lost enough time with them already. Why don't you fish it?"

"Shoot, I just might. Give me half a chicken and a bottle of bourbon, and I'll conquer the world."

"Ha! Whatever you say, buddy. I'll have to come up soon."

"Damn right, you do. I like it so much down there, I might be down sooner rather than later. I gotta go, I just got to the boat ramp, gonna go catch some Alabama buoys!"

Clay reorganized the shop after the hurricane of people had swept through the place. He ordered more inventory and sat back behind the counter, happy as could be. If he kept up this pace, he would be out of debt and in the green for the first time since he sold his dad's house. He could get his own place—it would need to be two bedrooms so Red could have his own room. Maybe Abi could even move back in. Then he could get a new truck, go on vacations; he could have a life with his family.

A car bounced over the potholes through the parking lot and parked next to the front door. Hank stepped out of the car with a suit and sunglasses on. "Clay Booker." He smiled as he walked into the shop. "Looks like you're busy this morning! Not busy enough, I'm afraid."

"Hank. How can I help you?"

"You can start by giving me four months' of payments."

"We both know I don't got that money."

"Well, that's too bad. Selling your dad's house only put off the wolves for so long. But guess what? We're back, and we're hungry."

"Get out before I put you on your ass again."

"You have thirty days to come up with the money Clay. I might just throw a party when we tear this dump down. I can't wait." Hank slapped an envelope from the bank onto the counter and strutted out of the shop.

CHAPTER 25

THE BANK CALLS

Clay fell back into his chair. It didn't matter if he was as busy as he was today for the next month, there was no way he could come up with that money. Just as things were looking up for him, he was slapped in the face by reality. He crumpled the legal paper into a ball and threw it into the trash, then paced back and forth in the shop. A picture of his proud, young father standing in front of the brand-new Buoy Bait and Tackle in the nineteen eighties hung on the wall. Clay examined it for a second, took it off the wall, and threw it across the shop as hard as he could. Without thinking, he grabbed his keys, left the shop without locking up, and sped out of the parking lot.

He sped down the road, his hand on the steering wheel with the tightest grip he could muster. He parked over two separate spots and slammed the door behind him. The liquor store was a stand-alone shack, not much nicer than his own shop, and he walked into the store angrily. An old man with thick glasses sat behind the counter. "Clay, haven't seen you in a while."

He walked directly to the whiskey aisle, without responding, grabbed a fifth of his favorite whiskey, then dropped it on the counter. "Is everything alright?" the man asked.

Clay said nothing, dropped a twenty dollar bill on the counter, unscrewed the cap as he left and took the largest swig he could muster. He continued driving with no set destination in mind. As he drove, he drank more and more. He didn't listen to anything on the radio, only sat in silence, the only noise was the gurgling of the brown liquor dropping into his gullet. Alone, he sped past hundreds of acres of pasture in the opposite direction of the Lake. It was a long, lonely road, lined with barbed wire fences so that nothing could get in or out. It had no end in sight; it just disappeared into the horizon. He felt as if there were no escaping this road. He tried to turn things around, but he was meant to travel it alone. It was over, and there was nothing he could do. What a joke it was that he thought he could get his life together. He was meant to be a loser and always would be. There was no saving his father's business, there was no saving himself. He laughed as he took another swig. *What a moron.*

He ended up back at the shop in a haze. Some people had finished their day of fishing when he raced his truck through the parking lot and around back to the barn. He sloppily pulled the doors open to the barn, the bottle still in his hand. There sat the boat in fine condition. "What a joke," he said to himself, before taking another swig from the bottle, but it was finished. "Fuckin' thing." He threw the bottle against the wall. It smashed into small pieces, and he rolled his way onto the boat, gripping anything he could to climb onto the deck. He hunched over, and rested his head on the steering wheel, then slammed it with the palm of his hand over and over again. "Dammit… dammit! Why'd you have to leave me? You would know what to do." He sat in silence for a minute and leaned back in the seat. "I should go sink this thing for good."

"Clay?"

"Abi…" He leaned his forearm on the steering wheel as he squinted at her silhouette in the doorway.

"What're you doing?"

"They're taking it away from me, Abi. It's over."

She climbed into the boat and sat next to him. She didn't have to ask him if he'd been drinking; it was obvious. "Taking what away from you?"

"The marina. The shop. Everything. I'm gettin' evicted."

"Well… how much do you need to pay them?"

"Four months' payment. It don't matter. I don't have the money, obviously. I don't have anything. Where's Red?"

"He's at school. It's Monday, Clay. C'mon, let's get you inside."

"No. No, I'm going to go sink this fuckin' thing for good." Clay went to stand up, but Abi slapped him across the face.

"You don't know what the hell you're talking about!" Clay held his face. He had been slapped plenty of times by Abi in the past, and it hurt just as much as he'd remembered. "You've finally begun to clean up your life. Red is as happy as I've ever seen him. You were turning back into the Clay I knew before your father died. And you know what had a big part in that? As stupid as it sounds—this boat." She pointed toward the lake glistening in the midday sunlight through the open barn doors. "That lake, and the freakin' bass that're swimmin' around it!" She wiped a tear from her cheek. "And you're willing to throw that all away just because of a bump in the road? Fine, do whatever you think is best."

"Abi, I—"

"I came over to bring you something, found it rummaging through some old boxes." She searched through her purse and placed an old topwater plug on the dash of the steering wheel. The lure had been white at one time, but now had a rust-orange tint to it. The paint was scratched off as if it were covered in battle scars.

"My pop's old lure."

"Yeah… I gotta go."

"Abi, no, please don't."

"I'm not mad, Clay. I understand what you're battling. But I think you need some time by yourself. I believe in you. You need to start believing in you. Forgive yourself." She rubbed his arm, got off the boat, and walked away.

Clay sighed and picked up the old lure. He ran his fingers over the scars, then touched his finger on the point of the treble hooks. "You would know what to do," he said to himself as he gripped the lure. His eye lids grew heavy, and the last thing he thought before passing out was what his dad always said, *the answer is always to fish.*

CHAPTER 26

THE ANSWER IS ALWAYS TO FISH

Clay woke to a stiff neck and a splitting headache after using the deck of the boat as a pillow. It was dark out, but the single light of the barn illuminated the room around him. His mouth was dry, and it made it hard to breathe. He groaned as he lifted himself up. Every part of his body ached. Looking at his watch, he saw it was ten o'clock at night. It took all the power he could muster to sit up and run his hands through his hair. "What did I do?"

The recollection of the day came back to him. His heart raced. "Abi's never gonna forgive me." He went to call her, but it was late, and he decided against it. He started to walk and kicked the lure on the ground with his shoe. He picked it up, and the words of his dad reverberated. *The answer is always to fish*. He squeezed the body of the lure, pressed his lips together and shook his head. "Then let's fish."

He stumbled into the shop, took a water from the small collection of drinks he offered in the fridge, and chugged it. All the boats were gone from the parking lot, and except the ringing in his ears, it was dead silent.

The picture of his Dad sat on the floor with shattered glass resting atop it. He stared at the young Redmond, eager to begin his new business. "I ain't gonna let you down, Pops," he said, as he swept up the glass.

He couldn't stand to be in the shack another second, so he walked outside. Night crickets chirped from the corners of the lot. The moon was full, and there wasn't a cloud in the sky. The moonlight reflected silver rays across the surface of the lake, broken by small, choppy waves from a slight northern wind. With his hands in his pockets, he walked up and down the empty docks, the wood creaking with each step. At the end of the dock, he sat down, his legs dangling over the water. It wasn't long before there was a disturbance on the water from a hungry fish. It was a quick sound, as though an apple had fallen from the sky and into the water. Then came another, and another. He stood and watched over the dark surface of the water. Whatever was out there was aggressive and hungry, and by god, Clay was going to catch it.

He walked as fast as he could to the barn. He did tell himself earlier that day he was going to take the boat out, he thought, but now he didn't plan to sink it. In a month, if he wanted to use this ramp, he would have to pay someone else to use it, anyhow. The bass were biting, it was a full moon, and he wasn't going to sleep anytime soon. He pushed open the door, backed his truck to the boat, and had it in the water in a matter of minutes. The moon was high in the sky and was just about as bright as the sun during the day. He didn't even need a light to tie on a wild, neon green prop bait with a propeller on the face and tail. He hoped it would make enough commotion at the surface to get those bass going. There was no need to run anywhere. He didn't even try to turn on the big motor; he dropped the trolling motor down right outside of the ramp and began to fish.

There was something soothing about being on the water at night. As he maneuvered into the basin in front of the marina, he paused for a moment and took a deep breath with his eyes closed. The croak of the frogs along with the crickets and breeze cutting through the tall reeds was a hypnotizing melody that soothed every inch of his psyche. His jaw relaxed, shoulders lowered, and heart rate fell. A sense of peace rose over him, and it seemed like everything would be alright in that time and place. The distinct pops of bass breaking the surface, feeding in the moonlight, brought him back to reality.

The neon bait left a streak of green, as if it had a long, disappearing tail, when it flew through the air. He could hear the water splash around the bait as he twitched it along the surface. It was a nice addition to the melody of the night. While paying attention to his surroundings more than his lure, a bass wrecked the surface, and Clay hooked up. It was a little guy and was caught and back in the water in a minute. He continued fishing, in no rush whatsoever, using the trolling motor to fish the edge of reeds until he was far from the ramp. The bass were biting, and just about anything he threw out there, as long as it was loud and obnoxious enough to be found in the dark, was demolished. It was one bass after another, and he couldn't wait to brag to Red about it. He wasn't sure if it was the fresh air, the fishing, the night sky, or a combination of everything, but the worries of the world had all but disappeared.

After catching three bass in a row, he sat down behind the steering wheel and propped up his feet. He'd left his phone at the shop, but the moon was high in the middle of the sky, and he figured it was just past midnight. The farther he got into the lake and away from everything else, the more stars he could see. He could almost connect the dots to make a largemouth in the sky. His own kind of constellations, the Lake O constellations. With his feet propped up, he became lost in the night with dreams of monster bass.

Mud slid between Clay's toes as he waded through waist-deep, murky waters. Thick fog surrounded him, and he could only see a few feet in front of him. Dreary cypress trees cut through the fog, long strands of moss draping their limbs and teasing the surface of unmoving water. A block-headed brown snake with tiger-like, dark markings and a thin neck wrapped itself around a fallen branch that was half submerged. As the snake pushed past, it slithered into the water and disappeared into the fog. Creatures just under the surface made a wake as they pushed through the water.

He continued to trudge through the mud, parting the fog as if he were swimming through it. The yellow eyes of an alligator glowed with an incessant stare. Clay stopped as the eyes grew closer. Its spiked tail moved back and forth, well behind its eyes, and was the only other thing out of the water. The dinosaur-like creature slithered past him, its tail moving in the same motion as the snake.

The fog cleared as he came to the sprawling base of a Cypress tree that was twice as wide as he was tall. The top disappeared into the trees as if it were a mountain rising to the heavens. Long, thick strands of green moss hung from the fog hidden branches, and Clay pulled on the moss to see if it was sturdy. As he raised his leg onto a tall root just under the surface, planning to find out what was in the sky, he

195

heard something in the distance. He paused and listened harder. It was the sound of someone working a topwater lure as it plopped through the surface. He had heard that sound a thousand times. It was the sound of a small metal ball bouncing around the inside of the lure as someone twitched it in. The sound echoed through the fog and off the trees. It felt as if the sound continuously bounced around him. Then it subsided, and for a moment, there was silence.

Intrigued, Clay made his way around the wide trunk. The fog cleared into an open basin, and a shadow of a man stood at the front of a bass boat. He was casting a topwater plug away from the big tree and toward three fallen trees stacked atop one another in a pyramid-like shape, similar to the base of a tepee. The topwater moved across the surface as if it were an injured baitfish. The shadow man reeled and worked the lure at the same time, causing the lure to move sideways in a sporadic motion. "Hey," Clay said. The man didn't answer, only cast his topwater plug out and twitched it back toward himself. "Hey!" Clay said, louder this time. No answer. The shadow man cast again. Picking up his pace, Clay ran through the mud and toward the front of the boat as fast as he could, tripping over himself as he went. It got deeper as he moved toward the shadow, and he stopped in chest-deep water. As he came around the boat, the shadow man lightened, and he saw his father. Dead still in the water, Clay saw his father take another cast. The sound of the topwater reverberated through the still air. "Dad?"

Continuing to work his topwater, Red looked down at Clay. "What're you doin' in the water, son?"

"I… I don't know."

Red reeled in his topwater as it came close to the boat, then cast again. "Well, you better figure it out. You got a lot goin' on."

"What are you doin'?"

"I'm fishin'. Exactly what you should be doin'."

Clay looked around. "There ain't any bass here, Pops."

Red continued to work the topwater to the boat when a sea monster from the depths exploded on the plug. It was as if TNT detonated on the topwater as he worked it in. Red's rod bent into a half circle, and he grunted as he pulled against the unseen monster on the end of his line. He fell to his stomach and pulled in a bass that was the size of his torso. Its stomach bulged, and distinct black markings covered its side but were obscured by a long, uneven scar. The dorsal fin and tail were serrated and uneven. As calm as could be, as if he caught colossal, crazy looking fish all the time, Red unhooked the bucket-mouthed beast and held him up for Clay to see. "Remember what she looks like. You're gonna need her."

"For what?"

He put up his rod and sat down behind the steering wheel. "Always remember, they lurk in the murk, son. Dirk doesn't have a chance."

"Dirk? What are you talking about?"

Red started the engine, and the sound of the motor gurgling echoed through the foggy basin. "You'll figure it out." He turned the steering wheel and idled into the fog. "They lurk in the murk, son. Remember that!" he said before disappearing.

"Pops?" Clay walked forward, toward where his Dad had disappeared. "Dad!" He began to run now, but there was a drop-off, and his body plunged into the depths.

He burst out of the water, and it was light out. The sun was just over the horizon and rising every second. Clay grabbed the side of his boat, gasping for air. He looked around; there were no cypress trees in sight. He was exactly where he fell asleep, only now in the water. As he climbed back in the boat, it dawned on him that there was an empty shop that needed every last penny it could acquire, and he was not there to get those pennies. He hadn't gone too far from the marina the night before, so he made it back within a few minutes using the big motor.

It was a similar scene to the day before. Boats were lined up to the road, and the parking lot didn't have any open spaces. The boat ramp was packed full, with no room to take his own boat out, so he parked it in one of the many empty slips, tied her down, and opened up the shop. It was bittersweet for Clay to see all the people using the marina. His dad would have loved to see it like this, he thought; even at the business's height, it was never this busy.

As the morning progressed, business slowed and most people got out on the water. Clay sat back behind the counter, his feet propped in the air, hands resting on his chest. He missed his dad, and seeing him in that dream made him miss him that much more. He looked around the shop. It had been the one constant throughout his life. Buoy's was always there for him, and it was going to be taken from him. "I'm gonna miss this place."

CHAPTER 27

SHOW UP AND WIN

Clay went through the storage in the dull light of the barn. With a slight smile, he looked through old things of his dad's that had been packed away for far too long. There were antique twitch baits still in the box, a few old baitcasters, lead weights, hooks, and old plastic lures of all kinds and colors. His dad's old topwater lure sat on the counter, and he held it once again.

His dad's words repeated through his mind. *The answer is always to fish. Dirk doesn't have a chance.* What did all that mean? Did it have a meaning at all? A tingle that began in his fingers ran chills through his body. *Dirk doesn't have a chance*, he heard his dad say again. "I beat him once, I can do it again," Clay whispered to himself as he stared at the lure. He put the lure at the top of his tackle box and zipped it closed.

Abi answered her front door to Clay holding a bouquet of sunflowers. "Clay?"

Clay smiled. "I was gonna call you, I just know you're busy in the mornings. And I know I messed up, I'm sorry you had to see me like that. It's just—"

"Stop. It's okay. I just don't need that in my life, and Red especially doesn't. And I'm not going to tolerate it."

"I get it, you're right. I'm done Abi. I promise. You two mean more to me than anything else in the world."

"I know." She smiled and gave him a quick kiss, which surprised Clay. "Whatever is happening or going wrong, we're a family. We can get through it together. You're not alone."

Clay smiled. "These are for you."

"I love them. You want to come in?"

"Sure. Where's your parents?"

"They went grocery shopping." Abi took out a vase and put the flowers in it. "But really, they go for all the free snacks they hand out. They're gettin' old."

"I have an idea to save the shop. It's a little crazy." They sat on the couch next to each other. "I wanted to know what you think."

"Well, go ahead."

"I think, with the help of Sherman, there could be some sort of tournament to save the shop."

"You mean you would make a tournament, like the Lake O Extravaganza?"

"No, a one-on-one tournament. Me versus Dirk. Two days."

"And how would that make you any money?"

"That's where Sherman comes in. He can take care of getting sponsors and setting up the tournament. As long as we can get enough sponsors to put up the money, I know I can beat him again."

Abi giggled and hugged him. "Then what're you waiting for? Call him, and let's get this thing going!" They clasped hands tightly, with passion, as if they would never let go.

Clay dialed Sherman. The phone rang half a time before Sherman answered.

"Well how-dee-do, Mr. Booker, nice of you to return my calls. I thought you were dead."

"I've had a rough day, pal. Afraid I got some bad news."

"Shit, what is it?"

"I'm late on my mortgage to the bank, and they're gonna take the shop away from me."

"You're kiddin' me? Them slimy bastards. I'm tellin' ya, every last one of 'em are crooks."

"I hate to ask this, but I need a pretty big favor from ya."

"Say no more my friend, I'll stroke the check right now. We ain't lettin' no bank take that place away. How much you need?"

"No, no. I ain't askin' for money. I got an idea. Me versus Wesley, two day tournament. If you'd be interested that—"

Sherman whistled through the phone, and Clay held it back from his ear. "That's the kinda fire I'm lookin' for, Mr. Booker! Count me in!" Clay could hear Sherman fumble his phone around, and he began to speak more quickly. "I'll take care of the sponsors, and we can sell tickets. Oh, I like the sound of this. Where's it gonna be, Lake Okeechobee?"

"I don't know, I was gonna ask you."

"Hmmm. Let's put the ball in Dirk's court. I know he ain't gonna back down from somethin' like this. I guarantee he'll be cocky enough to let you decide. All you gotta do is show up and win."

Thousands of people tuned in to a live online call between Sherman, Dirk, and Clay as it streamed on Sherman's website. Sherman acted as the mediator, like he was the referee between two heavyweight contenders. Live comments streamed in with all sorts of fishing jargon and hundreds of suggestions for different lakes that the viewers wanted to see them fish. Sherman squinted into his camera and moved it around. "Alright! Welcome!"

Clay sat in the back room of the shop dressed in an old hat and button-down shirt, using Abi's laptop because he didn't have one of his own. Dirk sat in what looked to be a high-end bait shop, with every last thing a fisherman would ever need. Perfectly aligned packets of soft plastics, hooks, lures, and weights dangled on shelves behind him. A large, mounted bass hung on the wall, along with a flag showing off all of his sponsors. He wore sunglasses and a black hat with more sponsors on it.

"Thank you, everyone, for tunin' in! My name is Sherman Puckett, and this is the official announcement of where this David versus Goliath story will take place. But before we get to the big question of which lake will be fished, let me introduce both of our competitors. To the left, we have three-time National Largemouth Series Champion, Dirk Wesley! And on the right, owner of Buoy's Marina, Bait and Tackle, and winner of Lake O Extravaganza, Clay Booker! Dirk, do you have anything to say to the folks before we get to the decision?"

He licked his mustache. "Yeah, Sherman, I'm just glad to be here. This should be good fun. I'm just excited to get out on the water. It's been a few days now, and I'm ready to catch some big'uns. Booker may have barely beat me on his home lake that he literally lives on, but there ain't another lake in this world that he can even compete with me on. I know it, everyone at home watchin' knows it. I'm not takin' this too seriously, because, quite frankly, I don't need to. That's why I'm leavin' this up to Clay. He can choose any lake in the world to fish outside of Lake Okeechobee, and I'll make him go home cryin' to his daddy."

"Clay? Anything to say to that?"

A spark flew up Clay's spine. "Yeah, I got somethin' to say. I beat 'em on Lake O fair and square. And I'm sure he will go out and catch some big ones wherever we choose. But he better catch five real big ones, because even though I don't have no national championships, don't mean I can't go out and catch five studs myself."

"Five buoys." Sherman said.

"Exactly."

Dirk scoffed at Clay's remark. "We'll see about that. What a joke."

"Alright! Before things get too heated, the big question of the night, where do you want to fish, Clay?"

"Kenansville Lake, an hour north of Lake Okeechobee."

"Kenansville? That little dump of a lake?" Dirk said.

"It's a small lake in the middle of Florida, great fishing," Sherman said. "I've caught many fatties there myself. Great choice, Clay!"

"But—"

"You said it yourself, Dirk! Clay made his decision! Kenansville Lake it is. And The Alabama Largemouth will make it happen. Alright, so just a quick overview of the rules. It will be a two day tournament at Kenansville Lake. Fishing will be done from seven a.m. to three p.m. the weekend before Thanksgiving, Saturday, November 21st and

Sunday the 22nd. Winner takes home a sweet cash prize of twenty thousand dollars and enough braggin' rights to last a lifetime. And one more thing, neither contestant is allowed to fish the lake beforehand, to make it as fair as possible. What man can go into a lake blind, and find the fish? Mano a mano. David versus Goliath. There will be announcements of merchandise that will go on sale very, very soon. There will be tickets to see the weigh-in live up for sale at midnight tonight as well! Limited seats, get them while you can! There will be food, drinks, games, all set up by The Alabama Largemouth dot com. As for the two competitors, do whatever you have to do to get ready. This is gonna be good people, don't miss it! Check The Alabama Largemouth dot com for updates!"

Clay smiled one last time, then closed the laptop and sighed in relief that was over. Abi and Red stood in the corner of the room. "That was awesome!" said Red, who was watching off his mom's phone.

"How did I do?"

"You did great!" Abi said.

"Yeah Dad, you told him who was boss!"

"We'll see."

CHAPTER 28

THE NIGHT BEFORE

For the next couple weeks, Clay continued with life as usual. He spent time with Abi and Red, went to church, and ran the marina. He began paying some bills back to the bank, but they continued to remind him that it was not enough.

Clay's beard hovered over scalding orange coals and grilling burgers. The breeze off the lake was cool and made for a pleasant evening. Red fished off the dock while Bill stood next to him, giving him pointers. Abi and Sue set up sides of mashed potatoes, collard greens, and coleslaw in the middle of a table outside. It was Abi's idea to have a cook out the day before the tournament began. She could tell Clay grew more anxious by the day, and she thought this might lighten his mood.

Clay watched Red and remembered he and his dad doing the same thing in the same spot. This was where he learned to fish, where he grew up. He was glad to see Red making some of the same memories before it was too late. Abi came up from behind him, and with the lightest touch, held his back. "Are those burgers almost done? I'm starving."

Clay kept his head down and focused on the burgers as he wiped his forehead. "Almost."

"Is everything okay?"

"Yeah, why?"

"You seem a little tense."

Clay looked up and smiled. "I'm sorry, just focusing on the burgers is all."

Abi frowned. She knew he was holding back, but didn't want to push him to bring it up. "Okay," she said in a tender tone, then kissed him on the cheek. "The burgers are burning."

Clay spun back around to smoke coming up from the grill. "Shit."

"Dinner's ready, y'all!" Abi said to Red, Bill, and Sue.

They all sat around the table, joking, laughing, and eating until they were full and lazy. Clay patted Red on the back and smiled. He was happy to be with his family, but there was a pit in his stomach that no amount of burgers could fill.

That night, Abi stayed with Clay. Red went home with Bill and Sue and planned on coming to the weigh-in the next day. She and Clay laid in his small pullout bed, and he was embarrassed he couldn't provide anything better.

"That was fun today," Abi said, standing in her pajamas.

Clay ran his hands through his hair as he rested his forearms on his knees. "Yeah, Red's growing up so fast. I can't believe it. You raised a great kid."

"Well, we have a lot more raisin' to do."

Clay stared at the ground and didn't respond. He thought about all the implications of the next two days. His palms grew sweaty, and he felt each vessel pump through his heart.

"What're you thinking?" Abi asked the silent Clay.

"About tomorrow. About my dad. The shop. You, Red. I can't lose… any of it. He's better than me. He really is. I got lucky before. Just so happened to run into some fatties. My entire life rides on this thing. And I don't know if I made the right choice in doing this. I'm scared, Abi." Abi loosened his clenched fist and intertwined her hand with his. "But I'll tell you one thing. I ain't just gonna go out there and quit. No, not a chance. He might be better than me, he might have better gear, more tackle, faster boat and better tech, but he doesn't have what I'm fightin' for. He doesn't have that fire burnin' in his heart that tells him you have to win, there ain't no other option. And I'm gonna do everything in my power to do just that, for you, for Red, for my dad, and for myself."

CHAPTER 29

DAY ONE

Clay rolled over in his uneven bed. It was three thirty in the morning, and he couldn't sleep. He groaned and got out of bed. There was a stack of boxes in the corner of the room he had already packed, and Abi laid curled in the blanket. He put on his jeans and work boots with a "Buoy's Marina, Bait and Tackle" cotton shirt. "I'll see you later," he said to Abi, who smiled when he kissed her on the cheek.

"This early?" she asked as she squinted at the alarm clock.

"Yeah, I have some things to get ready on the boat," he lied. The boat and all his gear had been set up for days, but he wanted to be alone for a while.

"Kick some ass," she said before falling back asleep.

Wiping the sleep from his eyes, he left the shop and got in his truck, which was already hooked up to the boat, ready for the ride to Kenansville Lake. He looked in his rearview mirror at the dim lights that illuminated the shop, and they grew smaller as he drove north.

His heart pumped, and his mind raced. What would he use today? Where were the fish at? How could he beat the number one fisherman in the world? Would he just embarrass himself and his family for nothing? Bluegrass played on the radio, and although there was more static than music, he turned up the volume to block out everything else. He tapped his finger to the beat nervously as he drove down the dark road two hours early.

He turned up the volume on the radio even louder. His heartbeat increased the second he turned off Fellsmere road and down the long, dirt road that led straight to the boat ramp at Kenansville Lake. The ditch beside it ran parallel as far as the eye could see. He drove slowly, his dim headlights helping him see a few extra feet in front of him. Each bump in the road shot back a memory of the crash, and there were many bumps. A deer jumped into the middle of the road, and Clay slammed on his brakes. He panted as the truck stopped just before the deer and it ran back into the woods. "Jesus." To his right stood the tall oak tree—the scene of the crash. The last memory he had of Kenansville Lake.

He stepped out of his truck. A deep scar ran sideways down the tree where the boat had ripped into its trunk. He ran his hand over the scar and took a few more steps to the side of the ditch, and then sat down. The water was calm in the moonlight, and the scene was calming. One would have never guessed that something so horrific happened there. Clay found himself squinting, trying to use the little light he had to see if there was any life pushing around the top of the water. He was just like every other sorry soul that had been captured by fishing, no matter the body of water, no matter the situation, he was always looking for the next fish to catch.

His hands had a slight shake to them. His entire livelihood rode on his shoulders, and he could feel the pressure intensifying every second closer to takeoff time. The pit of his stomach twisted, and without warning, he threw up off to the side.

A pair of headlights tumbled up and down the bumpy road in the distance. Clay stood up, and the truck stopped. "What the hell are you doin', brother?" a man asked with his window down. Clay couldn't see who it was but recognized Sherman's voice and his loud truck. The neon green lettering on the side glowed in the dark.

"Oh, nothin'. Just, uh, well, you know."

"I figured I might see you down here. You alright?"

"Yeah, I'm alright. Just figured I might get here a little early. I couldn't sleep."

"Shit, me neither. I ain't even fishin', and I'm nervous. If I were you, I'd be a mess."

"Thanks, that makes me feel better."

"I'm just kiddin', you're gonna do great. C'mon, buddy, follow me up, I'll show you the setup. I worked all yesterday getting this thing together."

Clay took one last look at the oak tree and the calm ditch behind it. In that instant, there was a disturbance on the moonlit water, and a large bass skied out of the water and splashed back in. He grinned and jumped back into his truck as he rumbled farther down the road behind Sherman. The first rays of light pushed over the eastern horizon as they pulled into the grass parking lot. A tall stage stood in the corner of the lot, looking fit for a rock band, with tall speakers on both ends. A large hanging banner with the sponsors and an oversized screen rested in the middle of it all. There were metal bleachers set up for more people than Clay expected, and off to the side was Sherman's boat on a trailer, advertising his business.

"Holy shit," Clay said as he got out of his truck. "You did all this?"

"Oh yeah, me and a crew of good ol' boys. Made a deal with the county and everything. I ain't playin' around, Clay." Sherman had two cameras in his hand as he rolled onto Clay's boat.

"What're you doin' with those?"

"Settin' up a live feed. People will be able to watch live on the big screen here and on my website as you fish. So don't say anything bad about me while you're out there."

"I can't make any promises."

"Whatever." Sherman stepped down from the trailer, out of breath. "Now, when people start showin' up, I can't take sides. But dammit, I hope you whip his ass."

"Gonna try my best, buddy."

People trickled in, and Clay began putting his boat in the water. Waiting on the shoreline, he rigged up for the day. Soon, the sun was up, and a crowd filled the stands. Three different news trucks filmed as they covered the story. "Dad!" He heard Red and popped up his head from the braid in his hands. Red ran down the steep hill, jumped on the boat, and almost tripped in excitement. "Hey, buddy! I thought you weren't comin' till later?"

"Me and mom woke up early."

"Is that right? Well I'm glad you're here buddy." Abi stood at the top of the hill, along with Bill and Sue. Clay waved as Red hugged him.

"Is that what you're gonna use?" Red asked as Clay tied on a swimbait with a skirt jig.

"I think I might start with it, what do you think?"

"I think you should use a topwater. That's what I would use."

"That ain't a bad idea, son. I'll rig one up."

Dirk still hadn't showed, and it was just about takeoff time. Sherman paced back and forth as he talked on the phone, sweat dripping from his forehead even though it was cool out. "Well, get here!"

A moment later, Dirk pulled into the parking lot much faster than he should have. The crowd of people spread out as he did a half circle and backed the boat down the steep ramp. Cameras flashed in the low light of the morning as everyone tried to get a good picture. He got out of his truck and waved at the crowd. He chewed gum with his mouth open as obnoxiously as he could. "Don't worry, the super-star is here! Ready to catch some bass!" He hopped in his boat, and a man with a "Team Wesley" shirt got into the driver's seat. Dirk had the boat in the water and was ready to fish five minutes before takeoff. Dirk sat behind the steering wheel, decked out from head to toe in sponsored gear. He put on his sunglasses and crossed his legs like he was relaxing in his living room. Clay paid no attention to him as he tied on his dad's old white topwater plug. The basin dropped fifteen feet below the ramp, and the crowd stood along the edge and peered down upon the two fishermen.

"Hey," Dirk said. Clay paid no attention to him. "You nervous? I would be if I were you."

Sherman stood at the front of the basin with a megaphone up to his lips. "One minute until takeoff!"

"You got a lot riding on this, huh? Your business, embarrassing yourself, your family. If that's even what you call whatever situation you got goin'. Your lady, what's her name? Abilene? She's cute, might have to take her out for a drink after I beat your teeth in over the next two days."

As Dirk talked smack, Clay looked to the lily pads at the base of the ramp. There was a large boil in the water from a hungry fish chasing its next meal. "I'd quit talkin' if I were you. Win or lose, remember we launched at the same boat ramp. You might be able to outrun me in your boat, but not on land." Clay idled forward before he could say anything else.

"Thirty seconds!" Sherman said. "Three... two... one!" Sherman waved a green flag as if it were a stock car race. Both threw their throttles down, and their bows raised to the sky. Dirk took off and in a matter of seconds was well ahead of Clay, who picked up speed slowly. The crowd cheered up and down the bank as they drove into the lake. Once in open water, Dirk trimmed his motor up and shot a rooster tail of water into the air as he did a few large circles, then took off. Clay didn't stick around for his antics and passed him on the way to his first spot. His plan was simple; he was going to fish the same spots he did with his dad years ago. He didn't know what else to do, but neither did Dirk.

The first area was a long patch of reeds that were thick in some spots and sparse in others. The bass would either be hugging the outside of a thick patch or would be in the middle of sparse stuff. It was a little early, but Clay hoped that they were into the reeds with a hard shell bottom in order to make beds for a short spawn in the fall. Clay was also hoping to find the big mommas around those beds. He studied the reeds with unwavering concentration, hoping to see them move not from wind or current, but from predators brushing against their stalks in search of their next meal.

The morning was calm, and there wasn't much movement anywhere. The sky was a light blue without a single cloud, which indicated a high pressure system and a hard day of fishing. But, the air warmed by the second, and that was a good sign. After several minutes of not catching anything with the spinnerbait but seeing some movement through the reeds, Clay decided to ditch it and try a slower moving flipping jig with a purple crawdad on it.

Dirk pulled into his spot not long after Clay began fishing, having been delayed by the donut show he put on for the crowd. He talked to himself as he studied his sonar fish finder. There were patches of red and yellow blobs along a drop off where lily pads grew. "This looks like a good spot. Y'all see that?" He pointed to the screen. "That's all fish. That's what we're lookin' for, folks. I saw this on the internet usin' satellite imagery, since there was no prefishin'. Looked like a good spot from the sky, and it looks like a good spot down below, too." He picked up a rod with a light colored spinnerbait. He had two monitors on the edge of his deck, so he could watch the fish finder as he cast. He whispered, "This is gonna be easier than I thought, there should be some studs around here, people. This shouldn't take long at all." He reeled with intent as he kept the rod tip low to the water and looked around for more signs of life.

"Oh!" He leaned his body back, and the rod bent over as he reeled in a small bass. It was only about a pound. He raised it up to the camera. "Good start, but no fish below three pounds go in Dirk Wesley's livewell." His eyes still fixated on the camera, he tossed the fish back in the water. "Not too bad of a start. Clay better watch out. I'm comin' for 'em."

The morning sun began to warm the air around Clay, who was in the same spot, now deeper into the long stretch of reed. He hoped it would turn on the bite because to this point, he hadn't caught anything. There wasn't much activity. The water was light brown, but clean and clear, like watered down sweet tea. He methodically cast or flipped to each patch of reeds, each point, each divot in the grass. It was a massive area to fish, and once he found them, they should be the right ones. He zoomed around the reeds, up, down, and side-to-side, as if he were navigating a maze. He stopped fishing until he saw something promising. The bottom was rocky and hard, just as they liked for making beds to spawn. The reeds were thick, but not so thick that the bass wouldn't be able to move around. Everything that needed to be there was there, except for one key component—bass. He remembered something his father said all the time, *Clay, you can't catch 'em if they're not there.* That echoed throughout his thoughts. It was hard for him to leave with everything looking as perfect as it did. But if there were no fish, there were no fish.

Just as he was about to abandon the area and move to the next spot, he spotted a thin group of reeds moving back and forth. Fishing had a way of doing small things like that. Just as it seemed like there were no fish to be found, and the couch and a nice cold beer sounded more and more enticing, a single bait fish spooked, or the reeds moved in a way that only a fish nudging them would cause, and Clay would have no choice but to stay and investigate. That small inkling was enough for Clay to stay, at least for a few more casts. He cast his creature bait out beyond where he saw the reeds move and bumped it across the bottom as it came into the brush. *Thump.* Clay grunted as the bass flailed out of the water in front of him. It was a good one, and Clay didn't say a word as he focused on getting the thing to the boat. The boat rocked to the left as he put pressure on the fish, but it darted to a thick patch of reeds. Clay turned the trolling motor and pointed the end of the rod toward the fish to give slack in the line. The line zigzagged through the reeds, and Clay's heart rate was that of a sprinter the last few meters of a race, but he didn't say a word as he moved his entire boat into the patch of reeds.

The trolling motor made a ruckus as the blades chopped through the dense stalks. The bass jumped from the reeds again, and Clay grabbed the braid line with one hand, then the bass with his other, almost falling into the water. He didn't blink once the entire fight. "Haha! That's a good start, right there!" he said to the camera. "That one's for you, Red! Got four more comin', buddy." He fist bumped the camera. It was a solid four-to-five pounder. Clay whistled through his teeth as he picked up his rod and marched back onto the front deck. "No time to waste, back to it."

Dirk worked the trolling motor with his foot on the pedal as he held his rod. He fished in the same spot he was before, doing big circles around lily pads, similar to the way Clay was around the reeds. He studied the fish finder attached to his deck as he cast. "I'm seein' plenty of fish down there, just no big mommas around. Dirk needs himself a big momma. A biiiig momma." He used the spinnerbait, but cranked it slowly, so it was in the lower part of the water column. "Now, I usually wouldn't use a spinnerbait when it's this cold out." He cast again. "But the water ain't all that cold yet. And with this high pressure movin' in, it's plenty sunny out, so those fish can spot that flash in the water from the silver and gold spoons on the end there—" He set the hook and reeled in another small bass. He flipped it out of the water with his rod and into his chest. "But these things just ain't gonna do it. Like I said, I need a big momma. This ain't it." He tossed the bass back in the water. "I gotta make a move. I don't got much of an idea where to go, so let's just go check some stuff out, see what happens." Dirk shrugged. "Little tour of Kenansville for the kids back home."

He zoomed out from the spot and drove around for a little while. He slowed down in the middle of a large cove and talked real low, like he was hunting. "Y'all see that?" With his entire hand, he pointed into the middle of the cove. "That slick on the water, that's a real good sign, right there." He talked with his hands quite a bit. "When a lot of fish congregate in one spot, it makes that oily slick that comes up to the surface, and it's a great indication that you need to stop what you're doin' and start fishin'." An aggressive swirl sent ripples through the water. "There they are, right dang there. That was a big fish that made that boil. Hopefully my buddy Clay is watchin' this as well. He could learn a thing or two about findin' fish. Now, here I'm gonna try to fish a little bit slower, something a bit more lackadaisical, I guess you could say. One of these big ol' worms could work out real nice, I think." His trolling motor self-deployed and was running before he took his first cast. "I'm gonna work this thing slow, just thump, thump, thump along the bottom." The rod tip moved slowly up and down, and he reeled every so often. "Yup…" He looked directly at the camera, smiled, and set the hook; it wasn't a little dinker. The rod bent over in aggressive tugs. "What did I tell y'all! That didn't take long. Who needs pre-fishin', anyways?" He laughed in a maniacal tone as he reeled in his catch. "C'mon, Momma! Come to Daddy!" He raised the rod with one hand and netted the fish with the other. "Boom! That's what I'm talkin' about!" He weighed the fish with his portable scale. "Five point eight pounds. That's what I'm talkin' about!" Dirk showed it off to the camera, then dropped it in the livewell. "Another one comin' up soon. Stay tuned, I'm gonna take this Clay character to school."

Just past lunchtime, and with one fish in the livewell, Clay needed to move. One decent sized fish wasn't going to do it for him. He looked out upon the long flat of reeds one last time for any little sign that he should stay. There had to be more big bass somewhere in here, but he couldn't find them. With only a few more hours to fish, he was in a rush. Not too far to the south was another spot he wanted to try. His engine rumbled and spit out smoke as it turned on, and he was on his way.

He bit down on his lip as he slowed, and, wasting no time, began to fish. Clumps of bulrush grew on high ground between the boat and shore, and made it appear that there were small creeks with flowing water around the clumps. He hoped that the bass would be staged in the protected water behind the bulrush, waiting for easy meals to swim by. He was so close to shore that cows grazed in a pasture in front of him. The smell of manure was strong in the air, and it reminded him of Okeechobee, making him feel at home. They mooed at him, as if to tell him that he was a stranger and shouldn't be near their land.

It didn't take long for him to hook up. It was a small one, but he tossed it in the livewell, where it laid next to the donkey that was twice its size. A few minutes later, he hooked up again, and not long after, he had five fish in the well. They weren't tournament winners, but at least he had five fish to weigh. He wondered what Dirk had.

"Boom! That's what I'm talking about! That thing almost snatched the rod right out my hand!" Dirk said as he reeled in another fish. He lifted a solid three-pounder out of the water. "That'll go in the well. I think I might just fish out the rest of the day here, folks." He sat down for a second, licked his mustache, and looked at the camera. "If I've said it once, I've said it a thousand times. Competitive bass fishin' ain't for the weak minded. This is hard work. I mean, it's a beautiful day out, but it's been hard fishin'. I figure I've probably cast a thousand times today—for what? Twelve fish. Whoo. I don't know if my counterpart knew what he was getting into."

The rest of the day was hard fishing for the both of them; nothing came easy. As two thirty came around, Clay didn't want to take any chances. He didn't have an amazing bag of fish, but that's why there were two days of fishing. He didn't want to get disqualified if he had engine problems again, so he decided to make his way to the ramp. He passed the three cypress trees that leaned together in a tepee formation, and he remembered the tall cypress that was cut in half by lightning right before his and his father's eyes. Each half laid in the water, mostly submerged. Chills went down his spine.

As Clay grew closer to the ramp, Dirk came in from the opposite side of the lake. People made their way from their seats to the edge of the shoreline once again. Dirk must've noticed because he pulled off and did donuts with his motor trimmed up again. The crowd cheered and clapped as his motor spit water to the sky. Clay slowed to an idle as he entered the small basin in front of the ramp a few minutes before three. He spotted Abi and Red in the crowd and waved at them. Red jumped up and down and waved fanatically to his father. *Fish until you can't fish anymore, son*, his dad's voice said to him. He peered at the lily pads in front of the ramp, took out his pole with the flipping jig, and tossed it out. Sherman stood behind some people with his arms crossed and shook his head, amused by his friend's resiliency.

With Dirk in the background, Clay focused on the pads in front of him, pulling his jig up and down through the pads. He paid no attention to the crowd around him or Dirk's antics. His line went slack and moved away from the lilies. He didn't feel anything; there was no hard thump. He reeled until the line was tight, then laid into whatever was at the other end of his line. His rod bent down to the water, and he took a step back as it peeled out line. The crowd cheered. It was a bass, and a good one at that. It jumped out of the water like a redneck SeaWorld stunt, and the crowd cheered louder. At a minute before three o'clock, Clay pulled the fish into the boat. It was his largest for the day, well over five pounds. He held the fish up so that the crowd could see it, and they applauded and whistled at the show that was put on before them. Dirk had stopped his antics to make it in on time. He had a scowl on his face as he idled into the ramp, no longer the center of attention.

Sherman stood on the stage alone, with the water scale in front of him. "Well, well, well!" he said into a microphone. "That was about the most interesting clock-in I've seen in a long time! What an awesome way to end the day for both contestants! Before we get goin', I'd like to thank every last one of you for comin' out and supportin' this tournament, and I'd also like to thank all the sponsors and vendors as well. I know it ain't easy gettin' out here, but as you can see, it's worth it. I could blabber on for a while, but let's get down to business. First up, the underdog, the owner of Buoy's Marina, Bait and Tackle, the catcher of buoys himself, Clay Booker! Come on up, Clay. Don't be shy."

The crowd cheered as Clay walked onto the stage. Sherman grinned. "That was some performance you put on for these folks just a few minutes ago, Clay. Did you know there were fish there?"

"Well, I didn't know for sure, Sherman. But I had a few extra minutes to fish, so I thought, why not? And it ended up working out, that's all."

"Tell us about your day out there."

"As y'all probably saw, nothin' came easy. It was a tough day, but I grinded it out best I could. I'm weighin' five decent fish that put me in a good spot, so I can come out tomorrow and win this thing. One thing's for sure. If I lose, it ain't gonna be from lack of effort."

"I like the sound of that. Show these people your two largest *buoys* for the day."

Clay leaned over and pulled out his two big fish. Both were fat and healthy, a good catch for any fisherman. "Those are some good'uns, brother! Toss 'em on the scale along with the rest, let's see what ya got…" The scale jumped around until it landed on nineteen point five pounds. "Nineteen and a half pounds! Not a bad first day, Mr. Booker. Not a bad first day at all. I think we're all lookin' forward to what you can do tomorrow. Next up, the number one bass fisherman in the world, the man that needs no introduction, Dirk Wesley!"

With his bag of fish in one hand, Dirk danced his way onto stage like he was listening to smooth jazz. "Those are some good dance moves you got there, Dirk."

"Well, thank ya, Sherman." He licked his mustache. "I could teach you sometime if you'd like."

"That's alright, my wife might get jealous. How'd your day go out there?"

"For only fishin' here once, ten years ago, and not taking this whole thing too seriously, I'd say pretty good."

Clay's ears perked, and he scrunched his eyebrows together.

"Never got on a real solid bite, but that's to be expected with this high pressure weather. Cold, clear days always make for a hard day of fishin'. I had some fun out there, caught some fish. I'm feeling good. I think tomorrow I'll blow this thing right out the water."

"Well, you sure did put on a show for us with those rooster tails out there. How'd you feel about Clay pullin' out a fatty while you were doing donuts?"

"Like I said before, Sherm, I ain't takin' this too seriously. This isn't the National Largemouth Series, yenno? That was cool, I guess. But it's gonna take a lot more than that to beat me. Nineteen pounds ain't gonna do it, my friend."

"With that being said, let's see what you got… twenty-two pounds even!" Dirk clapped as if he were on a golf course. "That puts you ahead of Clay by two and a half pounds—a solid lead. What's your plan tomorrow?"

"My plan is to go out and catch thirty pounds. There's some people out there that seem to think that my counterpart is as good, or even better than I am. I'm here to tell ya, ain't no one out there that can compete with me. I don't want to win by two or three pounds, I want to win by ten."

After the day one weigh-in finished, Red ran up and gave Clay the tightest hug he could muster. "That was so awesome. You were up there with those big bass. You are definitely gonna beat him tomorrow. And you caught that big one right there in front of everybody." He reenacted Clay catching his last bass as if he caught the bass himself.

"And then you just flipped it into the boat like it was nothin'! That thing was huge!"

"You did great, Clay," Abi said.

"Thank y'all. I don't know if I'll be able to come back, but at least I'm on the board. Go out tomorrow and see if I can't get some big boys."

"Some buoys!" Red said, still amped up.

"The great Clay Booker, ladies and gentlemen!" Dirk clapped slowly, and put his arm around Clay. "I gotta tell ya, I didn't think it would even be this close. I mean, I know you haven't fished too many tournaments—what is this your second? But in these two day tourneys, that's a big difference my friend. Ah, how rude of me." He licked his mustache. "You must be Abilene. It is a pleasure to meet you, darlin'. Dirk Wesley. I've heard a lot about you, beautiful."

Clay pushed Dirk's arm off of him. "Why don't you go find somebody else to talk to, buddy, before you get yourself hurt."

Dirk threw up his hands. "Hey, man. I just came over to say hello. That's all."

Red grasped his mom's shirt. Clay noticed the scared look in his eye and unclenched his fist. "I'll see you tomorrow, Dirt."

"That you will."

CHAPTER 30

THEY LURK IN THE MURK

Clay laid in the dark as he examined his ceiling with an un-wavering stare. The weight of the entire marina weighed on his chest. The clock read two a.m.—another night of no sleep. He was tired, exhausted, but there was no hope for rest. He told Sherman on the stage earlier that day that he was just out to have fun and go fishing. That was a lie. He said he wasn't nervous. That was a lie. He could go for a drink; that would ease his nerves and put him to sleep. Just one stiff drink wouldn't hurt. He needed a big fish, a really big fish. That was the only way he was going to be able to win. Dirk was going to get another twenty plus pounds; that was just about guaranteed. A grumble in the pit of his stomach moved quickly upward, and he ran to his toilet and threw up the little food he had been able to eat. His dad's voice rang through his mind. *They lurk in the murk, son… they lurk in the murk.* He missed his dad more than ever. He could've helped him win this thing. Dirk was right— a three pound difference might as well be twenty pounds when fishing against him.

The dream he had on the boat danced in his head. He had never fished that spot before, the spot with the tepee-like cypress trees, and who knew if there were fish there. He didn't think it looked all that fishy, but he didn't have many other options. He would try that first thing in the morning. It was right next to the boat ramp and could be fished in a matter of minutes. That's what he would do, his pops wouldn't steer him in the wrong direction.

Clay didn't get to the boat ramp as early as he did the day before. In fact, he showed up at the last minute. He wanted to project the image that he was confident about the day ahead of him. More people were there for the final day of fishing than had been on day one. Dirk had beat him to the ramp and waited in the water. This time, Clay made the dramatic arrival. His old truck's suspension squeaked as it bounced over the bumps, and the engine squealed as he backed the boat onto the ramp.

"There he is folks, just in time!" Sherman said over a microphone as he stood on the stage. He had fully equipped rods and a mountain of fishing tackle on the stage that he planned to give away in a raffle. "Just in time, in prime form! Ready to rip some buoys!"

It was another cool, dry morning. Clay held up his hand to acknowledge the crowd as he backed the boat into the water. Red and Abi stood at the front and waved. Clay blew them a kiss. Dirk stood on the front deck of his boat and zoomed through the lily pads on his trolling motor— where Clay had caught his big bass the day before. Clay got the boat all situated and was ready to go fish. Dirk idled past him and gave him a smug smile. Clay paid no attention.

As he looked at his watch, Sherman stood in the same spot he had the day before, waved his flag, and the second day was off to the races. Dirk took off, this time with no donuts or rooster tails, and left Clay in his wake. His boat had a 250 Mercury and was much quicker. It was a minute

ride for Clay, and as he slowed to the spot in his dreams—
the spot his dad swore by—he prayed he was right. He could
see the boat ramp from where he was, but it was small, as
were the people around the basin; he couldn't make out anyone. The water was just as his dad had said, how it always
was—murky. There wasn't much movement, and he didn't
have any confidence that there were fish there, but he didn't
have any other option. This had to work. This was *the* spot.

His dad was using a topwater in his dream, but this
wasn't a place to use a topwater. He put on a jig and
thumped it across the muddy bottom. It was an interesting
area to fish, with plenty to look at. He wondered how those
trees fell like that; it didn't make any sense. If it were wind
that made them fall, they would've fallen in the same direction. He couldn't come up with a logical conclusion as to
how they ended up like that. The large cypress that had split
in half from the lightning bolt rested easily in the water, de-
caying into the mud more each day.

A milky, green haze sat atop the still water, and the
only movement came from the ripples when Clay's jig fell
from the sky. He fished, and fished, and fished, and became
more discouraged by the second. It wasn't a large area to
fish, and he zoomed through it multiple times with no luck.
The only thing he saw were garfish on the surface, soaking
up the sun, and they looked more like dinosaurs than fish,
with their long bills, heavy-duty scales, and razor-sharp
teeth. Although they looked cool, they were not the preferred species to catch.

Clay reeled in his jig and sighed. "Dammit." There was
nothing there, he was sure of it. The clock was ticking, and
Clay felt the pressure mounting. What the hell was he to do
now?

Dirk went back to the open water ledge where he caught his big fish the day before. The fish hadn't moved. He stared at his depth finder. "Looky there, they're still here. Hopefully I didn't catch all the big'uns yesterday. Gimme that thirty pounds, baby. And I'm gonna do it on this." He lifted a large swim bait to the surface. "This is what's gonna get those big boys I'm lookin' for. Not gonna get a lot of bites, but when I do, mark my words, they'll be big. I ain't playin' around today, ladies and gentlemen."

The lure looked like a bluegill and had two treble hooks, one just below the mouth and one at the tail. In the middle, a break only connected by two pieces of plastic enabled the tail to move in a more natural motion. "I think the water is just warm enough for a hungry bucket mouth or five to swallow this thing whole."

He reeled in the bluegill slowly and kept it low in the water column. "It's warmin' up fast," he said as he took off his jacket mid-cast. "Good, that'll get these things eatin'." His rod laid on the deck, the bluegill lure still in the water. Then, as he tossed his jacket onto the console, the line tightened and his rod took off across the deck. Dirk dove on it, like a wide receiver reaching for the game winning catch, and caught it just before it plunged into the water. On his stomach, he raised the rod above his head as the fish dragged out line. He grunted as he came to both knees, then to his feet. The line went loose and fell to the water. The rod no longer bent. Dirk dropped to a knee, his face in his chest. His heavy breathing was the only thing that the crowd watching could hear. "That was her." He reeled in as fast as he could and put the lure onto the hook holder. He raised the rod over his head, then beat the rod on the side of the boat like a child having a temper tantrum. It broke in half after several blows, then he tossed it across the boat.

Dirk's hat had fallen into the water during his outburst, and his disheveled hair looked like a bird's nest. He exhaled as he looked around for his hat, then saw it floating away. Without saying anything, he used the trolling motor to race over and pick it up. He tossed the dripping wet hat back on his head like nothing ever happened.

Clay was on the move. With the leaning Cypress trees behind him, he didn't know where to go; he was just riding. This aimlessness was never a good thing. He ran parallel with shore, looking for some kind of life, some hint for him to stop. He drove for a while. *What would my dad do?* Then he saw an osprey far into what looked like a shallow meadow. But ospreys didn't hunt in the extreme shallows like that. There were multiple chunks of reeds and cattails that made winding, shallow creeks that went far back toward land. But there had to be some deeper water back there, or that osprey wouldn't be there. The question was, could Clay get back there without getting stuck. His depth finder read four feet, but the way the water acted, it appeared to get shallow quickly. He didn't have any other option. He jumped onto the deck and deployed the trolling motor, then peeked over the edge of the boat like he was looking over the edge of a cliff. He shrugged to himself and started for a creek in front of him that looked to be deeper than the others—but not by much. It was as if he were chasing skinny-water redfish during the flood tide in the low country of the Carolinas. He trimmed his big motor out of the water. The prop rotated in the wind. As he continued forward, the water became more and more shallow, but he could see where the osprey worked.

The water opened up and seemed like it got deeper; he just needed to get there. It was a deep hole the size of a small pond. The cattail patches were riddled throughout with spiderwebs connecting the reeds, waiting for an unsuspecting insect to fly through. He felt the hull scrape the bottom, then the blades on the trolling motor stirred up the mud. He was just out of casting distance, but there were wild swirls in the water, and the osprey whistled as it studied the water below him. There were a lot of fish in the hole, that was for sure. He raised the trolling motor and pushed forward another thirty feet, just close enough so his farthest cast could reach the fish.

His boat didn't sway back and forth in the water any longer; it was beached, and he knew it. But he could deal with that later— there were bass to be caught. With all his might, he flung a large, purple, pumpkin seed worm into the middle of the hole. He nudged it across the bottom, raised his rod, then reeled up the slack and repeated his technique for a few casts. Nothing. He cast again, still nudging it across the bottom. Swirls flailed the surface around his bait, and then he felt *the thump*. The bass on the end of his line tried to make a run, but there was no place to go, so it went up instead. It shook its head out of the water, revealing that it was a good one, the size of his two biggest the day before. It jumped, and jumped, and jumped again. Each time, Clay's heart skipped a beat, and he reeled him in as tenderly as possible. The fish tried to make a run for the reeds, but Clay put pressure on it and dragged him across the skinny water. As he got it to the boat, he pulled it out of the water. "That's what I'm talking about, right there! Whoo! I needed that. That's a buoy!" he said as he held it up to the camera.

Clay dropped the bass into his livewell and kept fishing. "Need four more of those. Four more of those, and I have a shot."

Dirk's hat dripped water as he continued fishing. He hadn't gotten another bite. He even tried to let the bluegill lure sit like he had before, but to no avail. The broken rod sat on the deck, and he switched to a worm. "When things are tough like this, this is where the good fishermen are separated from the great. I thrive in situations like this. I got a rod down, missed a giant, that ain't gonna stop me. Nooo, not gonna stop me. I've been here before, and I'll be here again. Just gotta keep fishin'. I wonder what my opponent is doin'. Probably fishin' right next to the boat ramp still. He ain't got no place else to go. Just gotta keep fishin'. I'll find 'em."

"Ope! Haha!" He reeled a fish through the open water; it stayed down the entire time. "He feels like a big'un! Ope, oh yeah, he's big… he's big!" He pumped his fist. "I'm on 'em now, baby! Look at that fatty! That's a Florida bass, right there." It was big, seven pounds. "And that's how champions do it, baby." He peered at the fish finder as he put the stud in the livewell. "Ope, looks like there's some down there right now—watch this."

In mid-stride toward the deck, Dirk cast the worm back out. He worked the bait for a minute, then hooked up again, this time bringing in a three pounder. He jumped around on the deck with the bass in his hand and laughed. "That's two in a row. What'd I tell ya? Gah-darn, that don't get old. I guess this little guy can spend some time in the well. Way it's lookin', won't take long to get an upgrade for her." This time, he took his time getting back to the deck, slugging a soda in front of the camera like he was doing an advertisement, then got back to fishing.

As the sun rose in the sky, the bugs came out of hiding. Gnats swarmed Clay's face, and although he tried to ignore them, he ended up constantly waving his hand around his face. "These bugs are brutal." He paused and lowered his rod to the water, then set the hook on another fish. "But if they're bitin', I ain't goin' nowhere. Ooo, it's another good one." He chuckled as he reeled in the fish. "Oh man." He got it to the boat, and it was just smaller than the other, but not by much. "Another good'un." The boat sat still, and he tried to tilt it back and forth but got no movement at all. "How the heck am I goin' to get out of here, is the question. Ehh, I'll figure it out later. Got more fish to catch."

"I wonder how many big ones are in here. Can't be that much more." He waved his hand in front of his face to scare off the bugs and cast. Three more were caught there, all three pounders, and as the osprey left, so did the bite. After multiple unsuccessful casts in a row, and the signs of life all but disappearing, Clay sighed. "Well, looks like it's time to try and get out of this mess." He rocked back and forth again. "Man, I am stuck." He chuckled. "What did I get myself into." With half the trolling motor blade out of the water, he put it on full blast in reverse and rocked back and forth. He got a little movement out of the hull, but not enough. "Shoot. SeaTow ain't out here, are they?" He looked toward the camera set up on the back of the boat. "Y'all think Dirk will come pull me out?"

The big engine sputtered once as he tried to turn it on. "This is not a good time to give out on me, darlin'. I need ya now more than ever." It sputtered again, then revved on. "Atta girl." With the trolling motor pushing the boat and the motor pulling it, Clay ran to the deck and swayed back and forth to loosen up the hull from the mud. At first, the boat didn't move. "C'moooon." He jumped from one side of the boat to the other, and it slowly began to back up. "There we go!" The motor spat up mud into the air, and it rained onto the boat and Clay. Covered in drops of mud, the boat moved backward through the shallows and soon picked up speed as it started to float again. Clay ran to the back as the boat reversed dangerously fast. He slammed the throttle into neutral and sat back in his seat. "Woo!" He raised his hands like he had won the tournament. "That was interestin'."

Dirk moved up and down the same ledge all day. He picked off a bass here and there, making as many casts as he could. "Cardinal rule numero uno, never leave fish to find fish folks. Not to mention, I ain't got much else to go on anyway. Just gotta keep hammering away." He switched to a swimbait, this one looking more like a six inch mullet than anything else. "I've never actually tried this thing before, but I figure with the five fish I got in the well right now, I'm winning this thing. No doubt about it. Unless my opponent catches thirty pounds, I'm good. The only thing that's gonna eat this bad boy is a monster. I mean a mud grouper baby. I'm gonna sip my soda and see if I can't pull out one of them these last few hours. Pressure is off me—all of it's on Clay." Dirk was arrogant and cocky, but he knew what he was doing. He fished hard and smart. There was no reason for him to waste his time trying to catch three pounders, if he wanted to break this thing open and show everyone there was no competing with him whatsoever, he needed a big one in the livewell. He didn't want to just beat Clay, he wanted to demolish him—and any question about whether Dirk was the best there ever was. After another hour of fishing, he leaned into one that didn't budge. "Oh man! I knew she was down there somewhere! C'mon, baby, come on in. I ain't gonna hurt ya. C'mon." The bass stayed down—it didn't jump once. With his open hand, he netted the fish, another seven pounder. "Another one! Gah-darn that thing is a fatty. That's what I'm here for folks, that right there! She looks to be about the size of the last! That should be the dot on the exclamation point people! Ain't no one can compete against me!" He dropped his rod and pounded his fist against his chest. "I'm the Largemouth King!" His voice echoed over the lake. "No one finds the fatties like I do! C'mon, baby! Woo!" He held the mouth up to the camera, hyperventilating as he spoke. "Look at the size of that bucket mouth, thing could swallow three of my swimbaits whole. It sure did try. If you wanna catch some monster fish, go with the swimbait. You won't regret it."

Slow moving, heavy, grey clouds moved in from the north, and soon the entire lake was covered in a shadow, along with calm, cool air. With an hour and half left to fish, Clay had his five-fish limit, with two big ones and three decent sized. It wasn't going to win him the tournament, and he knew it. He fished along the edge of a long line of reeds that formed jagged points into the water, but with nothing to show for it. Shivers traveled down his spine as the shadows dropped the temperature. A thick blanket of fog moved over the top of the lake, and visibility was low. More shivers crawled up his neck and onto his scalp. He heard his dad's voice again, as if he were whispering in Clay's ear. *They lurk in the murk, son.* A light rain began, and the drops rippled around him. He could no longer see a hundred feet in front of him. *She's there, you just gotta catch her.*

Just as his father did the last day they fished together, Clay sped through the lake with little-to-no visibility. He shot through the fog until his GPS said he was there. It was still raining ever so slightly, and it was dead silent. He studied all his different rods, considering what to use. *Use the topwater, Dad. That's what I would use.* His dad's beaten up, white topwater dangled on a rod that he hadn't touched the entire tournament. It reflected the little light there was and almost called his name. He squinted into the fog as he tried to find the tepee-shaped collection of cypress trees. The fog cleared as he entered an open basin and saw the trees on the other side of it. It was as if he were in a dome, surrounded by fog, but it was clear as day inside. Nothing had changed; the water was dirty and unmoving. An osprey whistled somewhere in the fog, then shot in and out of the dome. A brown, block-headed water moccasin slithered in front of the boat and disappeared into the thick. Clay twitched the topwater across the murky water. It was the only sound in the basin. "C'mon, Pops. I'm here. I'm using the topwater. C'mon." He wiped droplets of rain off his eyebrows and casted again, and again, and again. The clock ticked on. It was two forty-five. "One more cast." He tossed out the topwater as far as he could, but it was a bad cast, and the lure went in between two of the leaning trees and under the tepee. Just as the topwater landed, before he could twitch it once, a blackhole of an explosion sucked the lure in. The reel screamed as the fish took off between the leaning trees, away from the boat. "Holy shit!" Clay wasn't supposed to cuss on camera, but he couldn't stop himself. Fighting the bass with one hand, he zoomed the trolling motor as close as he could to the trees, but there were cypress knees scattered in front of him, and he couldn't go any farther. The line rubbed against the bark of a tree and began to fray. It was going to snap if he didn't do something fast. He jumped off the side of the boat with the rod in his hand. It was deeper than he'd thought, and his head plunged under as he struggled to keep the rod up and swim at the same time. He swam through the muck, head just above the surface as he tried to reel at the same time. He made his way around the trunk of one of the tepee cypress trees with his rod out of the water. He could see his braided line losing strands as it wrapped around the tree. This bass was smart; it didn't get that big by luck. The cold water splashed his face as he sloshed through the water, parting the money matts around him. He maneuvered through a jungle of Spanish moss that dangled from the limbs above. Finally, he untangled the line, and the bass did a mighty jump into the fog. It was the largest bass he had ever hooked. It had a long scar across its back, and its fins were serrated from years of battle in nature. The bass flailed, with only one of the treble hooks in the side of its mouth. Shoulder deep, and breathing with long, heavy sighs, Clay tried to stay calm, and warm, as he fought the fish that was now far from his boat.

Mesmerized, the crowd watched the video from the live feed on his boat. At first, it was just a shadow of a man, but then Clay appeared through the fog, swimming as fast as he could, with his rod between his teeth and a huge bass held above the water. It was a dark green, with black markings and a long white scar. At the same moment, Dirk rolled up to the ramp, but no one paid attention. The crowd cheered as Clay held up the fish like a trophy and climbed back into the boat. Clay peered at his watch as he practically fell behind the steering wheel, it was 2:55.

Shivering and cold, Clay started the motor, in too much of a rush to realize what had just happened. He took off into the fog. Sherman made his way to the front of the basin and studied the fog for any sign of Clay as time ran out. As the clock turned to two fifty-nine, Clay emerged from the fog and into the boat ramp's basin. Sherman couldn't do anything but fist pump. "Yes! Yes, atta boy!" he said, then looked around to see if anyone noticed him being unprofessional. The fog moved south as the weigh in began.

"Holy cow! What an unbelievable two days of fishin'!" Sherman said over the microphone atop the stage. "Can I hear it for these two fishermen? I mean, they really put on a show for us." The crowd cheered. Red stood on the bleachers and threw his fists in the air, cheering louder than anyone else.

"Can't ask for more excitin' fishin', people, really. Win or lose, both contestants should be proud of how they competed this weekend. Now, let's stop wastin' time and get down to business. This is for all the marbles, twenty thousand dollars, and a whole lot of braggin' rights."

"First up, you all know 'em—Dirk Wesley!"

Dirk strolled up with his bag full of fish. "What kind of goodies you got in there, Dirk?"

"I got some good ones, Sherm." He pulled out his two big fish, the two seven pounders.

"Yee dog, those are some healthy fish, right there. Stick 'em in the tank, let's see what kind weight you put up." The scale jumped up and around until it stopped at twenty-four point seven pounds.

Sherman whistled. "That puts you at forty-six point seven pounds altogether. How do you feel about that weight? Do you think it's gonna be enough?"

"I'm not overly happy about it, Sherman, if I'm being honest. My goal was to get sixty pounds, but it is what it is. I think that'll be plenty. I'm feeling real confident. I think I might use the twenty grand on a new dock for my vacation home up in Montana. The one I got now is a little ol—"

"Alright! Don't get too carried away. You haven't won just yet! If you could just stand off to the side there, let's get Mr. Clay Booker up here for a weigh-in!" Clay was wet from the chest down, and had a towel around his neck as he brought up his catch.

"Clay! What a day, huh?"

"Woo." He shook his head. "That was one of my more interestin' days of fishin', that's for sure."

"You wanna talk about going all out—this man trudged through the mud for a bass. You want this win bad, don't ya?"

"Shoot, I just wasn't goin' to let that stud get away whether it was a tournament or not. Just glad I got it to the boat." Clay's hands shook, not just because he was cold, but also because he was deathly nervous. He looked at Abi and Red in the stands and gave them a nervous smile. He didn't want to let them down. He didn't want to let his dad down.

"Well, you should be proud. You came out here and competed with the best—and put on a show while doing it. There's something to be said for that."

Clay nodded.

"Alright, this is it folks. Show us your big fish and toss them in the tank."

Clay lifted the five pounder out of the bag, then the massive one he had caught minutes before. It just kept going as he pulled it out; it was twice the size of his other. The crowd went wild.

"Now that's a buoy, right there!" Sherman said. "Holy moly."

Clay's entire arm shook as he dropped his fish into the tank to be weighed. He tried to control his breathing, but he couldn't. He was hyperventilating. As the scale jumped up, memories rushed through his head—he and his dad fishing off the dock at Buoy's when he was younger than Red; his dad tying knots under the kitchen light early in the morning before fishing; the wreck into the ditch; all the pain he caused his family, and the pain of losing the marina his dad had worked so hard for. It all rode on this very moment. Dirk stood in the background with his arms crossed. Sweat dripped from Clay's forehead as he held his breath.

"Twenty-seven point six pounds!" Sherman said. "That puts you at forty-seven point one pounds and makes you the winner of the Kenansville Classic!" Sherman grabbed Clay's wrist and held it in the air like he was the judge in a boxing match.

The man wearing a "Team Wesley" shirt ran to the side of the stage with a rules book and handed it to Dirk. Clay stood there emotionless. He couldn't believe he had just won.

"Wait!" Dirk walked quickly to the front of the stage, holding the book high in the air. "Wait! Wait one second now." Dirk squinted as he read the rules. "If an angler should leave his vessel to retrieve a game fish, and if that angler successfully brings the fish to the vessel, there will be a half pound deduction of the captured fish's total weight." He smirked. "So that puts Booker's total weight at forty-six point six pounds!"

Clay's heart dropped, and his legs felt weak. Sherman's shoulders dropped, and he looked down at the ground, then cleared his throat. "Um… one moment folks."

Sherman read the rules, and Dirk was correct. "I'm embarrassed to say this, ladies and gentlemen. But I have made a mistake. With the half-pound penalty, Clay Booker's total weight will be as Dirk previously mentioned, forty-six point six pounds. That makes Dirk Wesley the official champion of the Kenansville Classic." Sherman made himself smile and raised Dirk's wrist to the sky, but he gave Clay an apologetic look as he did it.

Dirk ripped his hand from Sherman's and fist pumped multiple times. Clay hung his head low and walked off the stage while Dirk jumped around. He'd lost much more than just the tournament.

A few days later, Clay sat on the floor of Buoy's with boxes stacked around him. The shelves were empty. He planned on selling the rest of his inventory to other local bait shops. He stopped what he was doing and leaned back on his hands as he studied the shop. He was going to miss it; this place was all he had ever known. He stood and grabbed a metal sign that read 'CLOSED PERMANENTLY', along with a hammer and a single nail.

Thanksgiving had been bittersweet for him. He ate with Red, Abi, and her parents. It was a nice dinner, and he tried to keep a smile on his face, but the defeat weighed heavily on his shoulders. He couldn't help but feel like he'd let everyone down. His phone rang as he held the nail between his teeth and positioned the sign against the pole. "Dammit," he mumbled around the nail. He punched in the nail with the hammer, then answered the phone. "Hello?"

"Is this the world famous Clay Booker I'm speaking with?" Sherman asked.

"The world famous loser."

"Ah, quit with all that. What're you doin'?"

"Currently, nailin' in a 'closed' sign. Gettin' ready to start emptyin' shit out of the shop."

"Well, tear that thing down. I got a few sponsors practically beggin' to give you money. All you gotta do is keep catchin' monsters on the pro tour."

ACKNOWLEDGMENTS

Writing, a lot like tournament bass fishing, is done alone most of the time. But publishing this novel has been nothing short of a team effort. I'd like to thank my father, Monty, for answering my countless questions on Largemouth bass fishing for he is much more of an expert on the subject than I am. Thank you to my literary editors Laura Graves and Randy Surles at The Story Ninja for showing great enthusiasm for Clay and his journey. They gave me ideas that I ran with, and made the story that much more crisp and exciting. I'd also like to thank my good friend Tom Walsh for reading over the manuscript, your unrelenting eye for detail is something that I admire and look up to. Thank you to Taylor Duran, you were the first to read the story when it was nothing more than one long unorganized idea. I appreciate your comments and helpful notes which were the catalyst to continue improving the story. And a big thank you to the Ebook Launch team for all the help during the publishing process from creating the book cover design to formatting the manuscript. Lastly, thank you to my mother, Lora. There were many times over the last few years I wanted to quit pursuing a career in writing. You reminded me that nothing worth while comes easy and pushed me to chase what I love.

ABOUT THE AUTHOR

Gage A. Peters is an independent author and angler from South Florida. *They Lurk in the Murk: Home Waters* is his debut novel and the first of a three book series. For more information on Gage and the *They Lurk in the Murk* series visit Gageapeters.com or follow him on Instagram @gageapeters.

Made in United States
Orlando, FL
21 April 2022

17031563R10150